SCHOLASTIC
Hot Topics

Football

ages 5-11 for all primary years

Peter Riley

SCHOLASTIC

Book End, Range Road, Witney, Oxfordshire, OX29 0YD
www.scholastic.co.uk
© 2012 Scholastic Ltd
123456789 0123456789

British Library Cataloguing-in-Publication Data
A catalogue record for this book is available from the British Library.

ISBN 978-1407-12710-1
Printed by Bell & Bain Ltd, Glasgow
Text © Peter Riley 2012

Peter Riley hereby asserts his moral rights to be identified as the author of this work in accordance with the Copyright, Designs and Patents Act 1988.

All rights reserved. This book is sold subject to the condition that it shall not, by way of trade or otherwise, be lent, hired out or otherwise circulated without the publisher's prior consent in any form of binding or cover other than that in which it is published and without a similar condition, including this condition, being imposed upon the subsequent purchaser.

No part of this publication may be reproduced, stored in a retrieval system, or transmitted, in any form or by any means, electronic, mechanical, photocopying, recording or otherwise, other than for the purposes described in the lessons in this book, without the prior permission of the publisher. This book remains in copyright, although permission is granted to copy pages where indicated for classroom distribution and use only in the school which has purchased the book, or by the teacher who has purchased the book, and in accordance with the CLA licensing agreement. Photocopying permission is given only for purchasers and not for borrowers of books from any lending service.

Commissioning Editor
Paul Naish

Development Editor
Holly Bathie

Editor
Julie Smart

Illustrations
Laszlo Veres/Beehive Illustration

Photocopiable page illustrations
Stephen Lillie/Beehive Illustration

Cover image
David Beckham © Michael Janosz/isiphotos.com/Corbis

Photography
Gareth Boden

Model-making
Linda Jones

Series Designers and cover design
Sarah Garbett and Mark Bryan

Acknowledgements
To Colin and Marilyn, who share in the pleasure and pain of following our team.

Images:

Page 3, Footballers © Lario Tus/shutterstock.com; page 4, Stadium © Albo/shutterstock.com; page 6, Children playing football © Fotokostic/shutterstock.com; page 9, Globe on a stand © 2011 Photos.com, a division of Getty Images, Model maker polaroids © Linda Jones; page 10, Model maker polaroids © Linda Jones; page 11, Vintage photo of boys playing football © istockphoto.com/Duncan Walker, Model maker polaroids © Linda Jones; page 12, Oxford v. Cambridge illustration © istockphoto.com/HultonArchive; page 16, Football equipment © istockphoto.com/val_th; page 17, Model maker polaroids © Linda Jones; page 18, Model maker polaroids © Linda Jones; page 20, World Cup mascot © imagebroker.net/SuperStock; page 24, Football stadium © istockphoto.com/kickers; page 25, Model maker polaroids © Linda Jones; page 27, Model maker polaroids © Linda Jones, Stadium lighting © Olena Simko/shutterstock.com; page 33, Model maker polaroids © Linda Jones; page 34, Model maker polaroids © Linda Jones; page 35, Sports physiotherapy © Capifrutta/shutterstock.com; page 41, Feet dribbling through cones © istockphoto.com/Mikkel William Nielsen; page 43, Goalkeeper diving for the ball © 2011 Photos.com, a division of Getty Images, Model maker polaroids © Linda Jones; page 48, Football in net © istockphoto.com/zentilia; page 49, Referee paraphernalia © Herminia Lucia Lopes Serra de Casais/shutterstock.com; page 50, Commentating equipment © istockphoto.com/cjmckendry; ; page 52, Match strategy © istockphoto.com/jokerproduction; page 57, Table football © istockphoto.com/Daniel Bendjy; page 58, Barclays Premier League logo © The Football Association Premier League Limited, MU v. Porto 2009 © Rui Alexandre Araujo/shutterstock.com; page 60, Crowd in stadium © Neale Cousland/Shutterstock.com; page 64 World football flag pattern © vichie81 /shutterstock.com; page 65, English flag © istockphoto.com/visual7, Welsh flag © istockphoto.com/visual7, Northern Irish flag © istockphoto.com/Yuriy Kirsanov, Scottish flag © istockphoto.com/visual7; page 66, World football © istockphoto.com/vahekatrjyan; page 67, World map © Volina/shutterstock.com; page 72, Italy v. France World Cup 2006 © Shaun Botterill/Getty Images; page 73, Football crowd © Ulrik/stock.xchng; page 74, Medals and trophies © Fotokostic/shutterstock.com; page 75, Model maker polaroids © Linda Jones; page 76, 2010 FIFA World Cup stadium, Capetown © Raphael Christinat/shutterstock.com.

Photocopiable page illustrations © Stephen Lillie/Beehive Illustration

All other images © Scholastic Ltd.

Contents

INTRODUCTION 4

PLANNING A PROJECT 6

THEME 1
The history of football 8

THEME 2
Kits, badges and mascots 16

THEME 3
Football grounds 24

THEME 4
Who's who in football 32

THEME 5
Football players 40

THEME 6
The game 48

THEME 7
The football season 56

THEME 8
Football around the world 64

THEME 9
Competitions 72

Introduction

The *Hot Topics* series explores topics that can be taught across the curriculum. Each book divides its topic into a number of themes that can be worked through progressively to build up a firm foundation of knowledge and provide opportunities for developing a wide range of skills. Each theme provides background information and three lesson plans, for ages 5–7, 7–9 and 9–11. Each lesson plan looks at a different aspect of the theme and varies in complexity from a simple approach with younger children to a more complex approach with older children. There are also photocopiable pages to support the lessons in each theme.

BACKGROUND INFORMATION

Each theme starts by providing information to support you in teaching the lesson. You may share it with the children as part of your own lesson plan or use it to help answer some of the children's questions as they arise. Information is given about the photocopiable pages as well as the answers to any questions which have been set. This section also provides a brief overview of all three lessons to help you select content for your own sessions.

The lessons

A detailed structure is provided for lessons aimed at children who are in the 7–9 age range. Less detailed plans, covering all the essentials, are given for the lessons aimed at the other two age ranges.

Detailed lesson plans

The detailed lesson plans have the following format:

Objectives
The content of all lesson plans is focused on specific objectives related to the study of football.

Subject references
All lesson plans show how they relate to specific curriculum-related objectives. These objectives are based on statements in the National Curriculum in England. They may be used as they are, or regarded as an illustration of the statements that may be addressed, helping you to find others which you consider more appropriate for your needs.

Resources and preparation
This section lists everything you will need to deliver the lesson, including any photocopiables provided in this book. Preparation describes anything that needs to be done in advance of the lesson, for example, making a football ground. As part of the preparation, you should consult your school's policies on all practical work so that you can select activities for which you are confident to take responsibility.

Starter
A starter is only provided in the more detailed lesson plans for ages 7–9. It provides an introduction to the lesson, helping the children to focus on the topic and generate interest.

What to do
This section sets out, point by point, the sequence of activities in the main part of the lesson. It may include activities for you to do, but concentrates mainly on the children's work.

Differentiation
Differentiation is only provided in the more detailed lesson plans for ages 7–9. Suggestions are given for developing strategies for support and extension activities.

Assessment
This section is only provided in the lesson plans for the 7–9 age range. It suggests ways to assess children, either through the product of their work or through looking at how they performed in an activity.

Plenary
A plenary is only provided in the lesson plans for the 7–9 age range. It shows how children can review their own work and assess their progress in learning about football. It is not related to other lessons, but if you are planning a sequence of lessons you may also like to use it to generate interest in future studies of football.

Outcomes
These are only provided in the lesson plans for the 7–9 age range. They relate to the general objectives. You may wish to add more specific outcomes related to the context in which you use the lesson.

Extension
This section is found in the lesson plans for 5–7 and 9–11-year-olds. It allows you to take the initial content of the lesson further.

Flexibility and extra differentiation

As the lessons in each topic are clustered around a particular theme, you may wish to add parts of one lesson to parts of another. For example, in Theme 4 'Who's who in football' 'you may wish to link Lesson 3 about running a club with Theme 6 'The game', Lesson 3 about the role of the manager in selecting the team.

In the lesson plans for 7–9-year-olds, differentiation is addressed directly, with its own section. In lessons for the other age groups, differentiation is addressed by providing ideas for extension work. However, the themes are arranged so that you may also pick activities from the different age groups to provide differentiation. For example, in a lesson for ages 5–7 you may wish to add activities from the lesson for 7–9-year-olds in the same theme.

Planning a project

You may like to use the topic for a class or school project culminating in a Football Day. This will need considerable preparation, but the result could be a very memorable event! This section provides some suggestions for activities leading up to the day and for a programme of events.

The activities suggested for the day are based on the lesson plans shown in the third column. Read through each lesson plan to work out how the activity can fit into the context of your Football Day.

Times are given for guidance only. You may want to lengthen or shorten an activity, depending on your circumstances.

FOOTBALL DAY (AGES 5–7)

Preparation

- If the children are to sing 'Come on football!' and perform the accompanying actions (Theme 9, Lesson 1), allow plenty of time for rehearsals before the day.
- If you would like a footballer to visit and present awards, contact them well in advance to make arrangements.
- Send a letter home asking parents or carers to help make medieval peasant costumes and to remind children to bring in their football kits. Collect spare kits for those children who do not have their own and who will not have a costume.
- Find books or posters showing scenes of medieval life to put on display as inspiration for those parents and carers who are making costumes.
- Let parents and carers know if you plan to include a footballer's meal as a feature of the day. You could extend this to an 'Eat like a footballer' project and start with a simple breakfast of unsweetened muesli and skimmed milk with fresh orange juice. Snack time could be a couple of oatcakes with soft cheese and lunch a chicken sandwich on granary bread with mixed salad, a low-fat yoghurt and a drink of the child's choice. This is a simple adaptation of a training day menu. More detailed menus can be found at www.mealplansite.com/sports-football-training-day.aspx and www.mealplansite.com/sports-football-match-day.aspx

	Time	Activity	Lesson plan	Pages
MORNING	15 minutes	*Cuju* activity	The history of football Theme 1, Lesson 1	8-9
	10 minutes	*Kemari* activity	The history of football Theme 1, Lesson 1	8-9/13
	60 minutes	Make a football ground	Football grounds Theme 3, Lesson 1	25/29
	30 minutes	Make your players	Kits, badges and mascots Theme 2, Lesson 1	17/21
	30 minutes	The team behind the team	Who's who? Theme 4, Lesson 1	33/37

	Time	Activity	Lesson plan	Pages
AFTERNOON	30 minutes	Making medals	Competitions Theme 9, Lesson 2	74-75/78
	20 minutes	Practising football skills	Football players Theme 5, Lesson 1	41/45
	20 minutes	Play a game	The game Theme 6, Lesson 2	50-51
	20 minutes	Meet a footballer	Football players Theme 5, Lesson 3	44/47
	10 minutes	Award ceremony	Competitions Theme 9, Lesson 2	75/78

FOOTBALL DAY (AGES 7–9)

Preparation

- If the children are to sing 'Come on football!' and perform the accompanying actions (Theme 9, Lesson 1), allow plenty of time for rehearsals before the day.
- If you would like a footballer to visit and present awards, contact them well in advance to make arrangements.
- Send a letter home asking parents or carers to help make medieval peasant costumes and to remind children to bring in their football kits. Collect spare kits for those children who do not have their own and who will not have a costume.
- Find books or posters showing scenes of medieval life to put on display as inspiration for those parents and carers who are making costumes.
- Let parents and carers know if you plan to include a footballer's meal as a feature of the day. Detailed menus can be found at www.mealplansite.com/sports-football-training-day.aspx and www.mealplansite.com/sports-football-match-day.aspx.

	Time	Activity	Lesson plan	Pages
MORNING	15 minutes	Cuju activity	History of football Theme 1, Lesson 1	8-9
	15 minutes	Football commentary	The game Theme 6, Lesson 2	50-51/54
	30 minutes	A football timeline	History of football Theme 1, Lesson 2	10-11/14
	30 minutes	My football club (Make a book)	Football grounds Theme 3, Lessons 1 and 2	25-27/29-30
	20 minutes	Rehearsal of football song and award ceremony	Competitions Theme 9, Lessons 1 and 2	73-75/77

	Time	Activity	Lesson plan	Pages
AFTERNOON	30 minutes	Making medals	Competitions Theme 9, Lesson 2	74-75/78
	20 minutes	Practising football skills	Football players Theme 5, Lesson 1	41/45
	20 minutes	Play a game	The game Theme 6, Lesson 2	50-51
	20 minutes	Meet a footballer	Football players Theme 5, Lesson 3	44/47
	10 minutes	Award ceremony	Competitions Theme 9, Lesson 2	75/78

FOOTBALL DAY (AGES 9–11)

Preparation

- If the children are to sing 'Come on football!' and perform the accompanying actions (Theme 9, Lesson 1), allow plenty of time for rehearsals before the day.
- If you would like a footballer to visit and present awards, contact them well in advance to make arrangements.
- Send a letter home asking parents or carers to help make medieval peasant costumes and to remind children to bring in their football kits. Collect spare kits for those children who do not have their own and who will not have a costume.
- Find books or posters showing scenes of medieval life to put on display as inspiration for those parents and carers who are making costumes.
- Let parents and carers know if you plan to include a footballer's meal as a feature of the day. Detailed menus can be found at www.mealplansite.com/sports-football-training-day.aspx and www.mealplansite.com/sports-football-match-day.aspx.

	Time	Activity	Lesson plan	Pages
MORNING	15 minutes	Cuju activity	History of football Theme 1, Lesson 1	8-9
	30 minutes	Make a badge Make a mascot	Kits, badges and mascots Theme 2, Lesson 3	20/23
	20 minutes	A football timeline (whole-class activity)	History of football Theme 1, Lesson 2	10-11/14
	30 minutes	Football around the world	Football around the world Theme 8, Lesson 3	68/71
	40 minutes	My football club (Prepare a short talk)	Football grounds Theme 3, Lessons 1 and 2	25-27/29-30

	Time	Activity	Lesson plan	Pages
AFTERNOON	30 minutes	Making medals	Competitions Theme 9, Lesson 2	74-75/78
	20 minutes	Practising football skills	Football players Theme 5, Lesson 1	41/45
	30 minutes	Football commentary	The game Theme 6, Lesson 2	50-51/54
	30 minutes	Meet a footballer	Football players Theme 5, Lesson 3	44/47
	10 minutes	Award ceremony	Competitions Theme 9, Lesson 2	75/78

Theme 1: The history of football

BACKGROUND

It is more than likely that round objects have been kicked around since the Stone Age and the game of *cuju* (see below) may have been played 7000 years ago. Records show that it existed in China in the Han dynasty (206BC – 220AD). A game called *kemari* was played in Japan in the Asuka period (538 – 710AD) and is still played today. Details of these games are featured in Lesson 1.

Football developed separately in Europe. It began in Ancient Greece with *harpaston*, a type of rugby football. When the Romans conquered the Ancient Greeks they adapted the game and called it *harpastum*. The Romans may have brought their version to Britain when they invaded. The game played in Britain in medieval times, however, was called mob football.

In Tudor times, the Headteacher of Merchant Taylors' School, Richard Mulcaster (1531–1611) developed a game with the basic rules we use today and called it football. Other schools began to play but each had its own set of rules. As many students at Cambridge University came from schools with different rules it was decided in 1846 to draw up a new set of rules. These were called the Cambridge Rules. In 1862 a teacher called Mr Thring wrote *The Simplest Game* which was developed into the rules set out by the Football Association (FA) in 1863. These formed the basis of the rules by which the modern game is played.

Women's football has been hampered by prejudice. The first women's game was played in 1895 and the year after 53,000 spectators watched a match at Everton. However the FA then banned women's teams from using Football League grounds until 1971. In 1993, the FA took over the running of women's football.

THE CONTENTS

Lesson 1 (Ages 5–7)
Cuju and kemari
The children learn about and play *cuju* and *kemari*.

Lesson 2 (Ages 7–9)
Football timeline
The children produce a timeline to show some of the important events in the history of football.

Lesson 3 (Ages 9–11)
The first league clubs
The children find out about the first league clubs in England and Scotland and learn their locations.

Notes on photocopiables

Kemari (page 13)
This page provides information about *kemari* for children to read with their teacher, and gives instructions on how to play. There is a picture which children can colour in, or use as inspiration to make a costume for themselves or a doll.

Football timeline (page 14)
Children need to cut out events in the history of football and place them on a timeline in chronological order.

The first league clubs (page 15)
The names and locations of the first league clubs in England and Scotland are listed alongside a map of Great Britain. The children have to mark the clubs in the correct place on the map.

Lesson 1: *Cuju* and *kemari*

Resources and preparation
- You will need: a globe.
- For *cuju*: tabards or sashes, an open space in which to play, four goalposts.
- For *kemari*: a ball for each pair of players, space for players to practise (up to 2 metres for each pair).
- Each child will need: a photocopy of page 13 '*Kemari*'.

What to do
- Tell the children that football was invented hundreds of years ago in China where they played a game called *cuju*, which means 'to kick a ball'. Show them China on a globe. Explain that they are going to learn how to play *cuju*.
- Divide the class into two teams of 12–16 players.
- Set out a pitch about the size you would normally use for children in KS1 and place the goals at either end.
- Tell the children that there is no goalkeeper and each team plays by passing the ball, running with it and shooting at the goal as players do today. Explain that there was a referee and in this game it will be you.
- Let the children play for about ten minutes.

Extension
Hand out the photocopies of page 13 and read about *kemari* with the children. Look at the pictures together. Ask the children to work in pairs or small groups and try to play. Finish by asking the children how *cuju* and *kemari* are similar and different to the football played today. The children could design and make a *kemari* costume for a doll using the picture provided as inspiration.

AGES 5–7

Objectives
- To learn about the origins of football.
- To play a version of the first football game.
- To develop skills of keeping the ball in the air.

Subject references

Geography
- Identify and describe where places are. (NC: KS1 3b)

History
- Identify differences between ways of life at different times. (NC: KS1 2b)

Physical education
- Travel with, send and receive a ball and other equipment in different ways. (NC: KS1 7a)
- Play simple, competitive net, striking/fielding and invasion-type games that they and others have made, using simple tactics for attacking and defending. (NC: KS1 7c)
- Remember and repeat simple skills and actions with increasing control and coordination. (NC: KS1 1b)

Art and design
- Investigate the possibilities of a range of materials and processes. (NC: KS1 2a)

Lesson 2: Football timeline

AGES 7–9

Objectives
- To learn about important events in the history of football.
- To locate these events on a timeline.
- To locate the ancient games and events in the history of football on a world map and globe.
- To learn when one or more local football clubs were founded by using ICT.

Subject references
History
- Use dates and vocabulary relating to the passing of time, including ancient, modern, BC, AD, century and decade. (NC: KS2 1b)
- Know about Britain and the wider world in Tudor times. (NC: KS2 10)
- Know about Victorian Britain. (NC: KS2 11a)

Geography
- Use atlases and globes. (NC: KS2 2c)

ICT
- Work with a range of information to consider its characteristics and purposes. (NC: KS2 5a)

Resources and preparation
- Make a timeline from 300BC to 2014AD. It should be long enough to accommodate the 28 events on page 14. Leave space for you to add more, such as the date your local club was formed, if you wish. Put the timeline around the walls of the classroom. Pin up a map of the world.
- Make 28 corner flags from triangular pieces of coloured paper (any colour will do) on which the children can write the date and name or event from the information on page 14. Attach them to cocktail sticks or similar before sticking to the timeline.
- You will also need: a football for the starter activity; information about your local club, including when it was founded; sticky tape.
- Each child will need: a photocopy of page 14 'Football timeline'.

Starter
Ask if anyone can play 'keepy uppy' and, if someone can, let them demonstrate their skill. Tell the children that this was one of the earliest forms of football, called *kemari*, and in this lesson they are going to trace the history of football and how it spread around the world.

What to do
- Point to the timeline and explain that in the Stone Age, 6,000 years ago, people probably kicked round objects about in some sort of game. You are going to look at games for which there is written evidence.
- Give out copies of photocopiable page 14 and ask the children to cut out the events in the history of football and arrange them in chronological order.
- Ask the children to name the first five events in the history of football and show on a globe where they originated. Ask the children to find the places on a map of the world.
- Remind the children about *kemari* and ask them whether it was the first football game. (It was the second.)
- As you go through the dates in the timeline you may like to add that King Edward II banned football. At the time of his reign, it was called mob football and was played between two large groups of people from different villages who ran through the fields and streets trying to get the ball into the opponent's goal, which was usually near the centre of the village. Other kings also banned football as they wanted people to

practise archery instead in case they were needed to fight for their country. You may also like to explain that early goalposts had no crossbar – a tape was attached to the top of the two posts.
- Give out the cut-out corner flags and ask each child to write a date and event from the timeline on their flag.
- Ask each child to bring out their flag, attach it to a stick and put it on the timeline.

Differentiation
- Less confident learners will need help with writing the information on the flags.
- More confident learners could try to work out what a game might have been like in 1870 by going back along the timeline from today and saying, for example, that shirts may not have been numbered (1939), the goalkeeper could handle the ball outside the penalty box (1912), there were no penalty kicks (1891), no goal nets (1890), no whistles for the referees (1878), no crossbar (1875) and no women's matches (1895).

Assessment
The children can be assessed on the ease with which they rearrange the information on photocopiable page 14 into a timeline.

Plenary
Let the children use the internet to find the website of one or more of your local football clubs. (You may wish to assess the suitability of a club's website before allowing the children access.) Encourage them to explore the club history section to find out when their club was founded. Extra flags could be made for these dates and stuck on the timeline.

Outcomes
- The children learn about some of the important events in the history of football.
- The children find out about the history of one or more local football clubs by using ICT.

Lesson 3 The first league clubs

AGES 9–11

Objectives
- To find out about the founder members of the Football League in England.
- To find out about the founder members of the Football League in Scotland.
- To locate the football clubs on a map.
- To use the internet to find out about the history of a favourite football club.

Subject references
History
- Know about Victorian Britain.
(NC: KS2 11a)

Geography
- Use atlases and maps.
(NC: KS2 2c)

ICT
- Work with a range of information to consider its characteristics and purposes.
(NC: KS2 5a)

Resources and preparation
- You will need: up to three footballs.
- If using the timeline activity from Lesson 2, you will need the resources suggested for that lesson (see page 10) and the children will need copies of page 14 'Football timeline'.
- Each child will need: a copy of page 15 'The first league clubs' and a map of Great Britain. They will need internet access.

What to do
- Ask the children if anyone would like to play 'keepy uppy' and let two or three children see how long they can keep the ball in the air. Tell the children that this was an early form of football played in Japan called *kemari*.
- You may wish to use the timeline activity from Lesson 2 as an introduction to the history of football.
- Tell the children that there were 12 founder members of the Football League in England. They were Accrington, Aston Villa (in Birmingham), Blackburn, Bolton, Burnley, Derby County, Everton, Notts County (in Nottingham), Preston, Stoke, West Bromwich Albion and Wolverhampton Wanderers. All of these teams still play in the league today except for Accrington who were relegated in 1893. They disbanded (or folded) in 1896. There is, however, a league club called Accrington Stanley which was founded in 1968.
- Tell the children that there were 11 founder members of the Scottish Football League but the only ones remaining today are Celtic (Glasgow), Dumbarton, Heart of Midlothian (Edinburgh), Rangers (Glasgow) and St Mirren (Paisley).
- Give the children copies of photocopiable page 15 and ask them to locate the towns and cities where the clubs play and mark them on their maps of Great Britain.
- Under supervision ask the children to use the internet to find the websites of the 16 clubs still in the league and go to the club history section to find out when they were founded. Let the children write the dates next to the names of the clubs marked on the map.
- If you have made the timeline, you could make some extra flags and add the names and foundation dates of these clubs.

Extension
The children could look up the website of their favourite club and find out when it was founded. If you have made a timeline, the children could add flags to show when their favourite club was founded and mark its position on the map. Some websites show photographs of early football teams that you may like to share with the class and discuss how football strips have changed.

Did you know?
John Heath of Wolverhampton Wanderers scored the first goal from a penalty kick in 1891.

THE INTER-UNIVERSITY ASSOCIATION
Oxford v. Cambridge

Theme 1
Lesson 1
Kemari

Kemari is a football game from Japan. It is like 'keepy uppy'. You can use your feet, knees, back and head to keep the ball off the ground. Pass the ball gently to the next player so that they can keep it off the ground, too.

The ball is called a *mari* and the player with the ball is called a *mariashi*.

The players of *kemari* dress up like this:

HOT TOPICS Football

Football timeline

Theme 1, Lesson 2

1991 Women's World Cup	**1890** Goal nets used	**1857** Sheffield FC founded, oldest club in the world	**1954** UEFA founded
1969 Women's Football Association formed	**1314** Edward II banned football	**1939** Players' shirts must be numbered	**1912** Goalkeepers not allowed to handle ball outside box
1100BC *Harpaston*, Greece	**1920** First women's international match	**1966** England wins World Cup	**1930** First World Cup tournament
1992 Premier League set up	**2014** World Cup in Brazil	**2004** Championship set up	**1895** First women's football match
1904 FIFA formed	**1681** Charles II removes ban on football	**1863** Football Association rules	**1878** Referees use whistles
1581 Richard Mulcaster starts school football	**30BC** *Harpastum*, Roman Empire	**1875** Crossbar fitted to goalposts	**1170** First football match report in England
206BC *Cuju*, China	**1888** The Football League formed	**1891** Penalty kick introduced	**AD538** *Kemari*, Japan

Theme 1
Lesson 3 The first league clubs

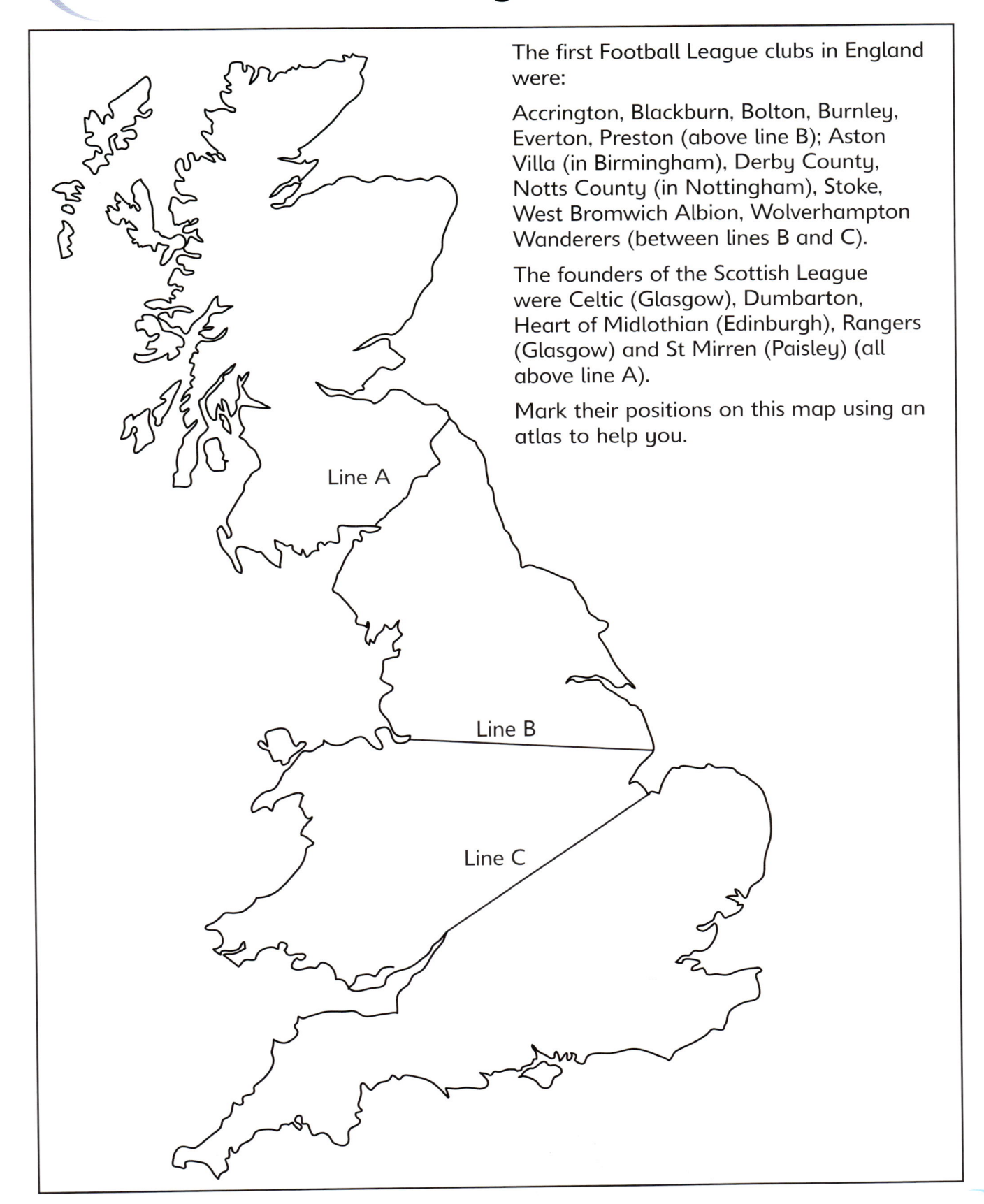

The first Football League clubs in England were:

Accrington, Blackburn, Bolton, Burnley, Everton, Preston (above line B); Aston Villa (in Birmingham), Derby County, Notts County (in Nottingham), Stoke, West Bromwich Albion, Wolverhampton Wanderers (between lines B and C).

The founders of the Scottish League were Celtic (Glasgow), Dumbarton, Heart of Midlothian (Edinburgh), Rangers (Glasgow) and St Mirren (Paisley) (all above line A).

Mark their positions on this map using an atlas to help you.

HOT TOPICS Football

2 Kits, badges and mascots

BACKGROUND

The first football teams did not have a kit. Football teams that developed from cricket teams played in their whites. Other teams, such as those associated with a church or factory, let their players wear what they could, but all teams tried to distinguish themselves in some way by wearing the same coloured cap, scarf or sash.

By 1870, teams began to have uniform kits. As many of the players were from public schools they wore the same colour as their school. The blue and white of Blackburn Rovers, for example, originated from Shrewsbury School (see www.historicalkits.co.uk/Blackburn_Rovers/Blackburn_Rovers.htm) while neighbouring Burnley had a whole range of colours and styles before settling on claret and blue, like Aston Villa (see www.historicalkits.co.uk/Burnley/Burnley.htm).

As football grounds developed and spectators paid to watch the game, the fans needed to be able to see their team clearly and simpler colour combinations, usually two contrasting colours, were used. Away shirts were introduced in 1890 and coloured socks were made compulsory around 1900. The players had to wear knickerbockers which covered their knees but after 1904 they could wear shorts.

Henry VIII had a pair of football boots made for him but in the early 19th century players used their work boots with steel toecaps. By the end of the century, boots had ankle protectors and leather studs. Since the 1940s, boots have been designed more for interacting with the ball, and less for protection. Modern boots give a great deal of control over the movement and direction of the ball.

THE CONTENTS
Lesson 1 (Ages 5–7)
Football kit

The children examine the parts of a football kit, perform an experiment on shin pads and design a strip for an imaginary football team.

Lesson 2 (Ages 7–9)
Football materials

The children make a football from a selection of materials. They test clothes for water absorbency, waterproof properties and warmth.

Lesson 3 (Ages 9–11)
Badges and mascots

The children learn about the components of a club badge and make one for their school. They learn about mascots and make one for their team.

Notes on photocopiables
Football kit: your team (page 21)

The children use the strip they have designed to colour in 11 players for their team. The team sheet is glued onto card, cut out and mounted in modelling clay for use in later lessons.

Investigating football materials (page 22)

This shows the equipment the children will need to investigate the properties of different materials. There is a chart where they can record their findings.

Club badge (page 23)

This page is an illustration of a composite club badge, showing all the possible features.

Lesson 1 Football kit

Resources and preparation
- You will need: two sets of kit for children to wear (one outfield player and one goalkeeper). It doesn't matter if they are out of date as long as they are clean. The kit should comprise shirt, shorts, socks and shin pads. The goalkeeper's kit should be green.
- You will also need: access to the school field or a green sheet fixed to a wall in the hall; a sand tray, football boot, shin pad. You may like to fill a bag (or sock) with sand to place inside the boot for extra weight during the shin pad investigation.
- Each child will need: a blank sheet of paper, a photocopy of page 21 'Football kit: your team', an A4 sheet of card, glue and a set of coloured pencils or crayons.

What to do
- Show the children the two football kits. Make sure that everyone knows the names of each item of clothing. Ask for two volunteers to try them on and run around. Ask the other children what would happen if the shirt was a thick, woollen pullover. (It would be heavy and make you feel hot and tired.) Ask what would happen if the shorts were long, stiff trousers (difficult to move and hot) and the socks were short (unable to wear shin pads so might get hurt).
- Give the children a football boot, a shin pad and a sand tray and ask them how they could be used to show the protection a shin pad provides. Smooth the sand flat. Drop the boot onto it and then remove to reveal the stud marks. Place a shin pad alongside the marks and drop the boot again from the same height onto the pad. Remove to reveal a fainter imprint in the sand.)
- Take the class out onto the school field and ask the two children wearing kits to run some distance away from you. Ask the class which child is most difficult to see. (Alternatively, have the children stand against a green background in the hall.) Encourage the children to think about the importance of colours when designing a football strip (to make the team stand out from the pitch and the opposing players). Why do they think a goalkeeper's kit is often green? Let the children draw an outline of a player on a blank sheet of paper then draw in and colour a football strip. They could cut out the players and compare the strips against a green background to see which ones are the easiest to see.

Extension
Hand out photocopies of page 21 and let the children copy their strip design onto the ten outfield players. They can think of a design for the goalkeeper, too, and colour him in. Glue the sheet to a piece of A4 card. The players can then be cut out and mounted in lumps of modelling clay to display.

AGES 5–7

Objectives
- To examine the materials used for a football kit and relate them to their use.
- To perform a simple scientific investigation.
- To design a strip for a football team.

Subject references
Design and technology
- Learn about the working characteristics of materials. (NC: KS1 4a)

Science
- Think about what might happen before deciding what to do. (NC: KS1 Sc1 2c)
- Recognise when a test or comparison is unfair. (NC: KS1 SC1 2d)
- Make simple comparisons and identify simple patterns or associations. (NC: KS1 Sc1 2h)

Art and design
- Ask and answer questions about the starting points for their work and develop their ideas. (NC: KS1 1b)
- Learn about visual elements including colour and pattern. (NC: KS1 4a)

Lesson 2 — Football materials

AGES 7–9

Objectives
- To investigate the materials used in football.
- To relate the properties of the materials to their uses in the game.

Subject references

Design and technology
- Learn how the working characteristics of materials affect the ways they are used. (NC: KS2 4a)
- Investigate and evaluate a range of familiar products, thinking about how they are used. (NC: KS2 5a)

Science
- Know that it is important to test ideas using evidence from observation and measurement. (NC: KS2 SC1 1b)
- Carry out a fair test or comparison by changing one factor and observing or measuring the effect while keeping other factors the same. (NC: KS2 Sc1 2d)
- Compare everyday materials and objects on the basis of their material properties. (NC: KS2 Sc3 1a)
- Learn that some materials are better thermal insulators than others. (NC: KS2 Sc3 1b)

Resources and preparation
- For the starter, you will need: materials for making a football such as cloth or a plastic sheet for the outer cover and spongy material, straw or raffia for the stuffing.
- If possible, arrange for all the children to wear a full football strip (either their own or from the school team kit). Failing that, you will need: one complete kit, including goalkeeper's gloves, for children to look at.
- For the experiments you will need: squares of material from a football shirt and shorts, a cotton shirt or blouse, a woollen pullover and a tracksuit; a bowl, a measuring cylinder, paper towels, containers for water. (Children's families may be able to supply old items of kit to cut up.)

Starter
- Tell the children that footballs in the past were made from a wide range of materials such as animal skins (fur inside), linen and leather stuffed with hair, moss, cork - anything that people could find.
- Show the children a range of materials and challenge them to make their own football and assess its chances of surviving a game.

What to do
- Let the children put on their football kits and compare them. They will notice differences in colour and design and you may like to talk briefly about how they make each team recognisable and easy to see.
- Point out that the materials used for most football shirts are similar as they are designed to prevent the wearer getting hot and sweaty. Look at the labels in the shirts to see if they are made of polyester. Show the children a cotton shirt and a woollen pullover. Ask how they could perform an experiment to see which material holds the most water. One test would be to take three samples of the materials of equal size. Immerse them in water, remove and hold up until they stop dripping, then squeeze the water out of each one into a bowl. Use a measuring cylinder to find the volume of water retained by each material.
- Ask the children about other items of kit such as tracksuits and training wear. Show them some examples. Explain that players often have to play and train when it is raining. Ask the children how to find out which material lets the least water through. They could place squares of football shirt, tracksuit material, cotton and wool on paper towels, pour the same amount of water onto each then measure the size of the water mark on the paper towel. The results could be photographed for a display.
- Ask the children what players do when they come off the pitch if they are substituted. Encourage them to think about putting on clothes to keep warm. Hand out photocopies of page 22 'Investigating football materials' and ask the children how they could use the equipment illustrated to compare how well different materials keep in warmth. Let them write down their ideas first, then test them. They should think about wrapping each container tightly in a different material so there are no gaps, using equal volumes of warm water, recording the temperature of the water at the beginning and after a set period of time (say 15 minutes).

Differentiation

- Less confident learners will need help to follow the sequence of activities in testing water absorbency and waterproofing properties. They will also need help in organising their ideas for the investigation on warmth.
- More confident learners could measure the temperature of the water at five-minute intervals for 20 minutes and produce a bar graph of the results.

Assessment

The children's answers and willingness to contribute to planning experiments can be assessed. The ideas written on the photocopiable sheet can be used as evidence of attainment.

Plenary

Let the children share the results of their investigations and draw conclusions about how the properties of the materials help footballers when they play and train. The children could look at a pair of football boots and identify the different materials. Look together at some goalkeeping gloves and think about how the material helps the goalkeeper make a save (padded to absorb the impact of a ball, sticky to improve grip, water resistant, tough).

Outcomes

- The children can use a range of skills to observe and measure in experiments.
- They can relate the properties of materials in a football kit to their uses in the game and in training.

Did you know?

The first time players wore shirts with their names on their backs was in the 1992 League Cup final.

Lesson 3 Badges and mascots

AGES 9–11

Objectives
- To understand the meaning of the symbols in a club badge.
- To use the symbols to devise a new badge for the school team.

Subject references

History
- Find out about events, people, and changes studied from an appropriate range of sources of information including ICT-based sources. (NC: KS2 4a)

Design and technology
- Generate ideas for products after thinking about who will use them and what they will be used for, using information from a number of sources including ICT-based sources. (NC: KS2 1a)
- Communicate design ideas in different ways as they develop, bearing in mind aesthetic qualities, and the uses and purposes for which the product is intended. (NC: KS2 1d)

Art and design
- Question and make thoughtful observations about starting points and select ideas to use in their work. (NC: KS2 1b)
- Collect visual and other information to help them develop their ideas, including using a sketch book. (NC: KS2 1c)

Resources and preparation
- Familiarise yourself with the websites mentioned in the lesson plan. Check that you will have access to the internet for the lesson.
- Each group will need: match-day programmes from your local football team showing the club badge, photocopies of page 23 'Club badge', coloured crayons and a selection of fabrics for making either a mascot doll or a life-size mascot.

What to do
- Tell the children that all football clubs have a badge or crest. It may have developed from the town's coat of arms or the original organisation involved in the foundation of the club; it may have elements of the two. The badge is usually displayed on the front of the programme, or just inside, and can provide further evidence of the club's history.
- Visit this website about basic heraldry and look briefly at the meanings of the colours, lines, shields, beasts, birds and other symbols (called charges): freepages.genealogy.rootsweb.ancestry.com/~jkmacmul/heraldry/index.html
- Analyse the components of the badge belonging to your local football club.
- Let the children analyse the badges of their favourite clubs.
- Tell the children that they are going to design a badge for the school team. To help them, show them the following website which provides detailed information on the badges of many local football clubs: www.footballcrests.com/uk-clubs.php
- Look at a few examples on the whiteboard to show children how a wide range of elements can be added to give a club a specific identity. Encourage them to think about the name of your school as well as local history or landmarks.
- Give out photocopies of page 23 and let the children use the websites as inspiration. Groups of children could work together to create a new school team badge. The design could be placed below the example of a coat of arms shown on page 23.

Extension
- Many clubs have a mascot. There are examples for children to see at: www.footballmascots.co.uk
- The children could decide on a mascot or submit their own designs and the winning mascot chosen by a class vote could be made into a life-size costume for someone to wear. Alternatively, up to six groups could each make a mascot.

Theme 2
Lesson 1 Football kit: your team

HOT TOPICS Football

21

Theme 2 Lesson 2: Investigating football materials

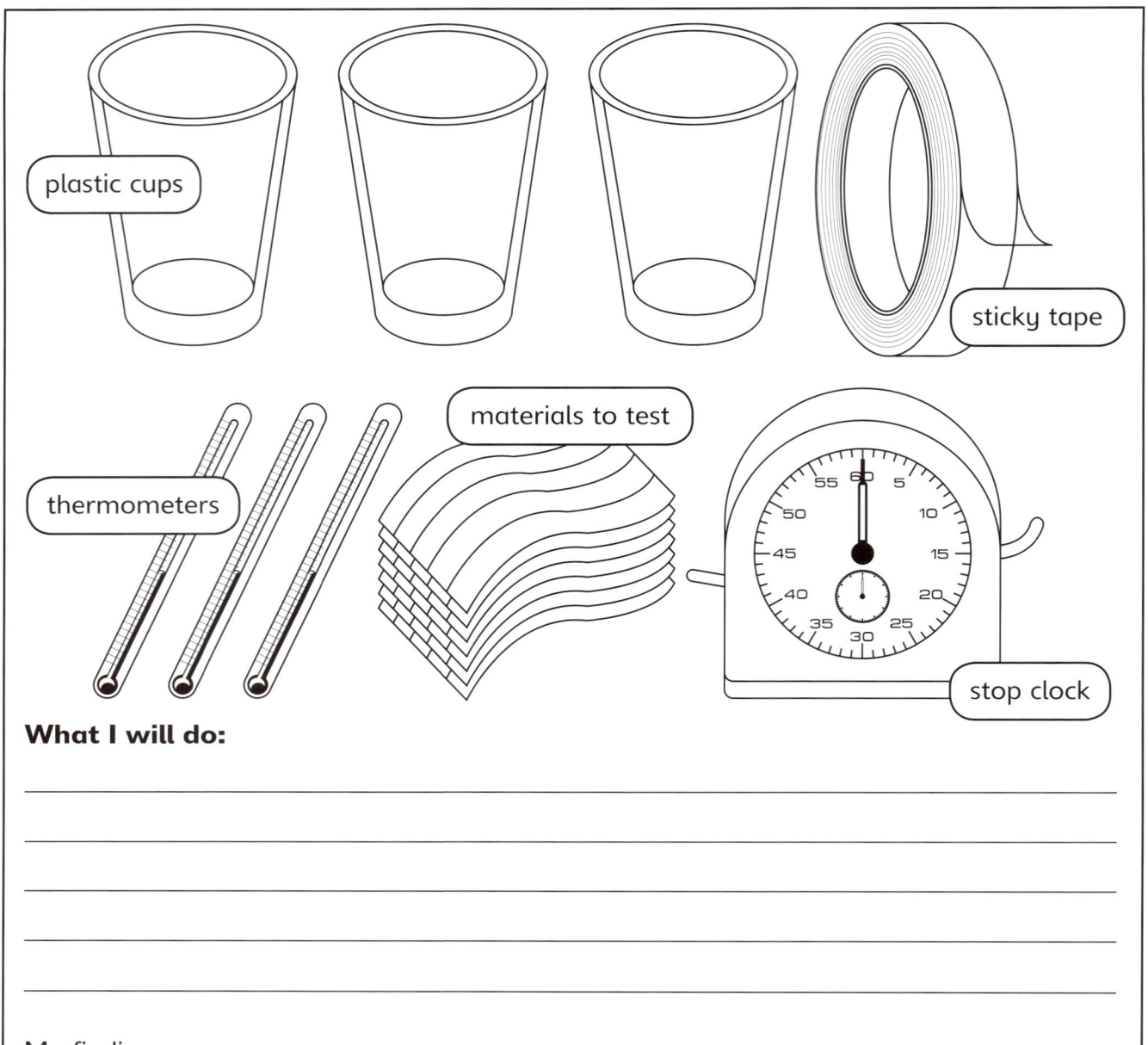

What I will do:

_____
_____
_____
_____

My findings:

Material	Start temperature (°C)	End temperature (°C)

Theme 2 Lesson 3 Club badge

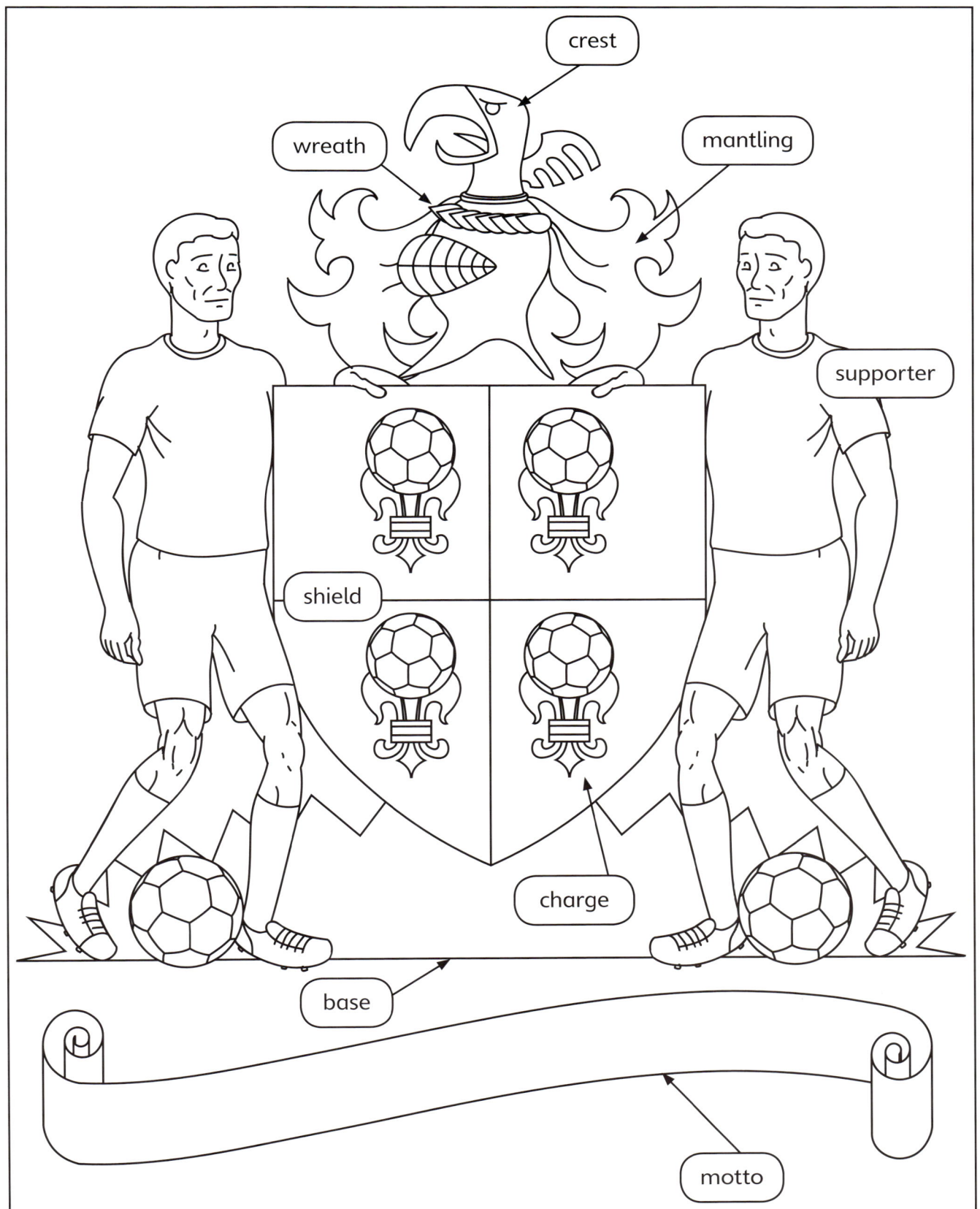

3 Football grounds

BACKGROUND

Football clubs originally played in parks or on cricket or rugby grounds but as their popularity grew they needed their own grounds.

Archibald (Offside Archie) Leitch was an architect who became famous for designing football grounds. His early work included industrial buildings and his football stands were like giant sheds. The first stadium he designed was Ibrox Park in Glasgow, for Rangers, and his first stand in England was at Sheffield United's Bramall Lane. This is still the oldest football stadium in the world at which professional football is played. Over 40 years he designed all or part of more than 20 football grounds in the United Kingdom and Ireland.

The first purpose-built football ground was Goodison Park, Liverpool, the home of Everton FC.

The features and dimensions of a pitch are shown in yards (still used in football commentaries and reports) and metres at:
www.knowledgerush.com/kr/encyclopedia/Football_(soccer)

THE CONTENTS
Lesson 1 (Ages 5–7)
Making a football ground
After visiting a football ground, or using secondary resources such as photographs, television recordings or websites, the children use a range of materials and objects to make a model football ground.

Lesson 2 (Ages 7–9)
Floodlights and big screen
The children make a model football ground. They investigate electrical circuits and make floodlight arrays and big screens for the model.

Lesson 3 (Ages 9–11)
Finding your way to the ground
The children use a map to find their way to a fictitious football ground, then use small-scale maps to find the way from school to the local football ground. They use the internet to find different football grounds and the routes to them. Any children who have travelled to away games could share their experiences.

Notes on photocopiables
A football ground (page 29)
This page shows an aerial view of a football ground with its major features labelled. You can use it to generate ideas about suitable materials and objects for making a model football ground.

Floodlights and big screen (page 30)
This page has pictures of six different circuits (series and parallel) for the children to build and investigate. It shows how to use bulbs to light a big screen and floodlights for the model ground.

Finding your way to the ground (page 31)
A fictitious map of a small town is provided for the children to practise finding their way to the football ground. The children then use their map-reading skills on a real map featuring their local football ground.

Lesson 1 Making a football ground

Resources and preparation
- Contact your local club to arrange a visit when the children can walk around the ground and buildings. You will need to organise this well in advance. Ask if they can supply a map for the children to use to identify the parts of the ground. Alternatively, this website www.englishheritageprints.com/football_grounds_from_the_air/photo/9133.html offers aerial views of various grounds around the country. You may like to select a lower league or non-league ground as it shows the parts of the ground more clearly than a large stadium.
- You may find this website useful for ideas: www.modelfootballstadiums.com/case-studies/goldstone-ground.php
- You will need: different-sized cardboard boxes for stands, cardboard to fold to make open terraces, straws (for goalposts, corner flags and barriers on open terraces), green paper or card and white paint (for the pitch), old tickets, graph paper (to make seating plans).
- If you made players in Theme 2 Lesson 1, you can use these but you will need to make the pitch large enough for two teams. You will need plenty of helpers to supervise the construction of the football grounds.

What to do
- Ask the children to describe a football ground and make a drawing on the whiteboard based on their suggestions.
- Hand out photocopies of page 29 and compare it with the one you have drawn.
- If possible, visit a football ground with the children and use a map to identify the various parts.
- Show the children the selection of objects and materials and ask them to suggest how they could be used to make a model football ground.
- The children should use green paper and white paint to mark out the pitch before they build the ground around it.
- Let the children work together to make one or more football grounds. They could have slightly different features.

Extension
- The children could make a seating plan for a small stand using a grid on a sheet of graph paper. They should label the rows A to D, starting at the bottom, and number the seats 1–10 along the rows. Give children a reference, such as A7 or C4, and see if they can point to the seat. Show the children some old tickets. Let them use them to design their own tickets, featuring seat rows and numbers, for their model stadium.

AGES 5–7

Objectives
- To observe the parts of a football ground.
- To plan a model football ground.
- To select materials and objects and use them to make a model football ground.
- To understand how people are given seats in a stand.

Subject references

Design and technology
- Generate ideas by drawing on their own and other people's experiences. (NC: KS1 1a)
- Develop ideas by shaping materials and putting together components. (NC: KS1 1b)
- Assemble, join and combine materials and components. (NC: KS1 2d)

Geography
- Use fieldwork skills. (NC: KS1 2b)

Mathematics
- Read and write numbers to 20. (NC: KS1 Ma 2 2c)

Lesson 2: Floodlights and big screen

AGES 7–9

Objectives
- To assemble two different kinds of circuits and observe them to understand how they work.
- To work together to make structures to house the circuits in a model football ground.

Subject references

Science
- Construct circuits, incorporating a battery or power supply and a range of switches, to make electrical devices work. (NC: KS2 Sc4 1a)
- Investigate how changing the number or type of components in a series circuit can make bulbs brighter or dimmer. (NC: KS2 Sc4 1b)
- Investigate how to construct series circuits on the basis of drawings. (NC: KS2 Sc4 1c)

Design and technology
- Plan what they have to do, suggesting a sequence of actions and alternatives, if needed. (NC: KS2 1c)
- Measure, mark out, cut and shape a range of materials, and assemble, join and combine components and materials accurately. (NC: KS2 2d)
- Carry out appropriate tests before making improvements. (NC: KS2 3b)

Resources and preparation
- Contact your local club to arrange a visit when the children can walk around the ground and buildings. Ask if they can supply a map for the children to use to identify the parts of the ground. Alternatively, use the websites featured in the resources and preparation section of Lesson 1 (on page 25).
- If you wish the children to make model football grounds as a starter activity, follow the suggestions for Lesson 1. If you wish to install the lighting and big screen that children make in this activity you may need to build the football ground on a larger scale.
- Each group will need: three bulbs in mountings, a 1.5V battery, a switch, seven wires with crocodile clips.
- The children will also need: boxes, kitchen roll tubes, cardboard, tracing paper, rulers and pencils, scissors, sticky tape or glue. They will need help making holes in the cardboard so that the bulbs fit in the various structures they make.

Starter
- Take the children to visit a local football ground or show them aerial views of a range of football grounds on the whiteboard. (See website recommended in Lesson 1 on page 25.)
- Let the class work together to make a model football ground. It should be big enough to accommodate the floodlights and the big screen that the children make.

What to do
- Ask the children what they know about floodlights at a football ground. They may be in rows along the top of the stands or on pylons at the corners of the ground. Tell the children that sometimes a light bulb burns out during a match but all the other bulbs keep shining. This gives a clue as to how the bulbs are wired.
- Give them copies of page 30 and look at how the electrical components are arranged in diagram A. Ask the children to assemble the circuit and switch it on.
- Ask the children to assemble circuits B and C and switch them on.
- Ask the children if they noticed any changes in the bulbs as the circuits increased in size. The bulbs would have become dimmer as more were added to the circuit. Unscrew a bulb from one of the circuits and ask the children to switch it on again. They should see that the bulbs do not light up. Remind them that to make this a scientific experiment they should repeat it to check the result. Ask your classroom assistant or voluntary helpers to remove a bulb from the circuits made by the other children. The bulbs should not light. Explain that this kind of circuit is called a series circuit.

- Ask the children to assemble circuits D, E and F and see if the bulbs change as the size of the circuit is increased. All the bulbs should stay bright.
- Unscrew a bulb from circuit F and ask the children to switch it on again. The two remaining bulbs should light up as brightly as before. Explain that this kind of circuit is called a parallel circuit.
- Remind the children what happens when a bulb goes out in an array of floodlights and ask them what kind of circuit they think is used (a parallel circuit).
- Look at the remaining diagrams with the children and challenge them to make a big screen or an array of three floodlights to fit onto a stand roof.

Differentiation
- Less confident learners could make a circuit with one bulb and a big screen structure to stand it in. The children could draw a football scene onto tracing paper and colour it in to represent the screen. Screens could be installed at either end of the pitch.
- Some children could make arrays of floodlights to fit on top of the stands.
- The most confident learners could make floodlights on supports for the corners of the ground.

Assessment
The children can be assessed on how easily they assemble their circuits from the diagrams and how well they answer questions about what they observed. They could also be assessed on how well they work together to make the various structures for the football pitch.

Plenary
Darken the classroom then ask the children to switch on their lights. They can observe how well they light the pitch and how well the screens provide an illuminated picture.

Outcomes
- The children assemble two different kinds of circuits, make observations on them and understand how they work.
- The children work together to make structures to house the circuits in a model football ground.

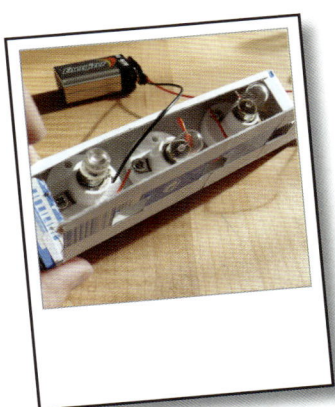

Lesson 3 — Finding your way to the ground

AGES 9–11

Objectives
- To know the location of the local football club.
- To produce directions to reach the club from school.
- To use the internet to find locations.
- To assess information provided about travel in football programmes.

Subject references

Geography
- Use maps at a range of scales. (NC: KS2 2c)
- Use secondary sources of information, including aerial photographs. (NC: KS2 2d)
- Use ICT in geographical investigations. (NC: KS2 2f)

English
- Speak audibly and clearly, using spoken standard English in formal contexts. (NC: KS2 En1 1e)
- Identify the gist of an account or key points in a discussion and evaluate what they hear. (NC: KS2 En1 2a)
- Obtain specific information through detailed reading. (NC: KS2 En2 3c)
- Use print and ICT-based reference and information materials. (NC: KS2 En2 9b)

Resources and preparation
- Contact your local football club to arrange a visit so that the children can walk around the ground and buildings. Ask if they can supply a map for the children to use to identify the parts of the ground.
- You will need: copies of page 31 'Finding your way to the ground' and access to maps.google.co.uk/maps?hl=en&tab=wl
- Each group of children will need: maps of your local area, a fixture list, an atlas and the support of a helper. They will also need a football programme containing away travel details. The programmes could either be from the same club but for different games so that they show different travel arrangements, or they could be from different clubs to enable comparisons of how they give fans travel advice.

What to do
- Ask the children the way to their local football club from school. Remind them that people use maps to find their way. Give them copies of page 31, a map of an imaginary town, and ask them to find two ways from the school to the football club.
- Hand out maps of your local area and see if the children can find your school on them. Now challenge them to find the local football club. Ask the children how they could use the map to find their way to the club. The children could work in groups, taking turns to write down instructions.
- Find your area on the website and zoom in on it. Switch to the satellite version as the football ground will be easier to see. Use the map on the website to check each group's directions on how to reach the football ground.
- Show the children the fixture list of the local club and point out the away games. Ask them to use the atlas with their partner to find the destinations on the map. See if they can work out which is the nearest fixture and which is the furthest away.
- The children could then use the website to explore a town where an away fixture is to be played. Let them zoom and scan to find the rectangular shape of the football pitch and its surrounding ground. They could assess how easy or difficult it might be to reach the ground through the town.
- Any children who have been to an away match could share their experiences with the class.

Extension
Give each group a football programme and let them find the section about travelling to the next away game. Using the Google Maps® website, let them follow the instructions on how to travel from one club to the next and say how easy they were to understand.

Did you know?
The first football league game played under floodlights was in 1955 at Portsmouth's ground, Fratton Park.

Theme 3
Lesson 1 A football ground

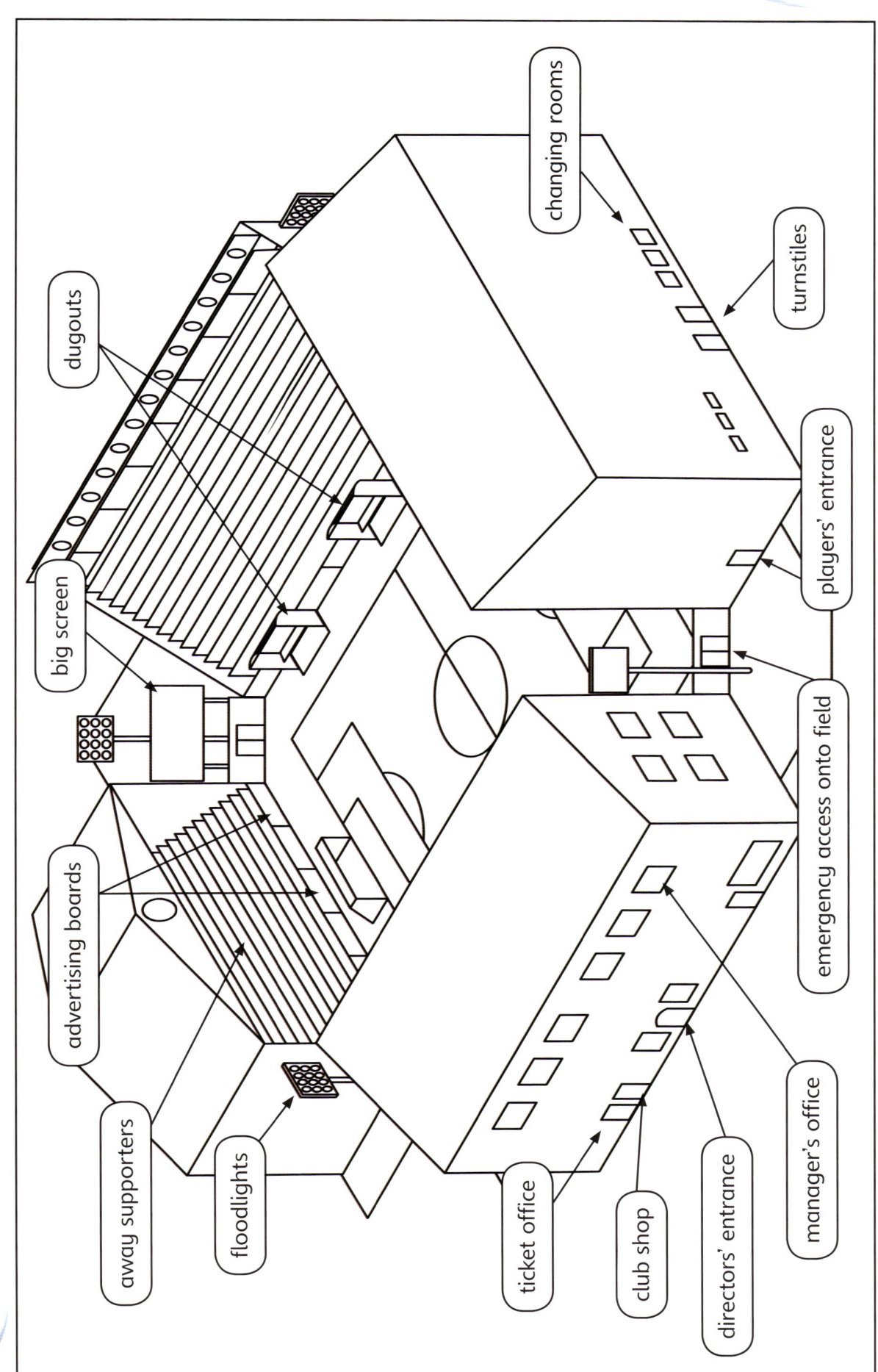

Theme 3 Lesson 2: Floodlights and big screen

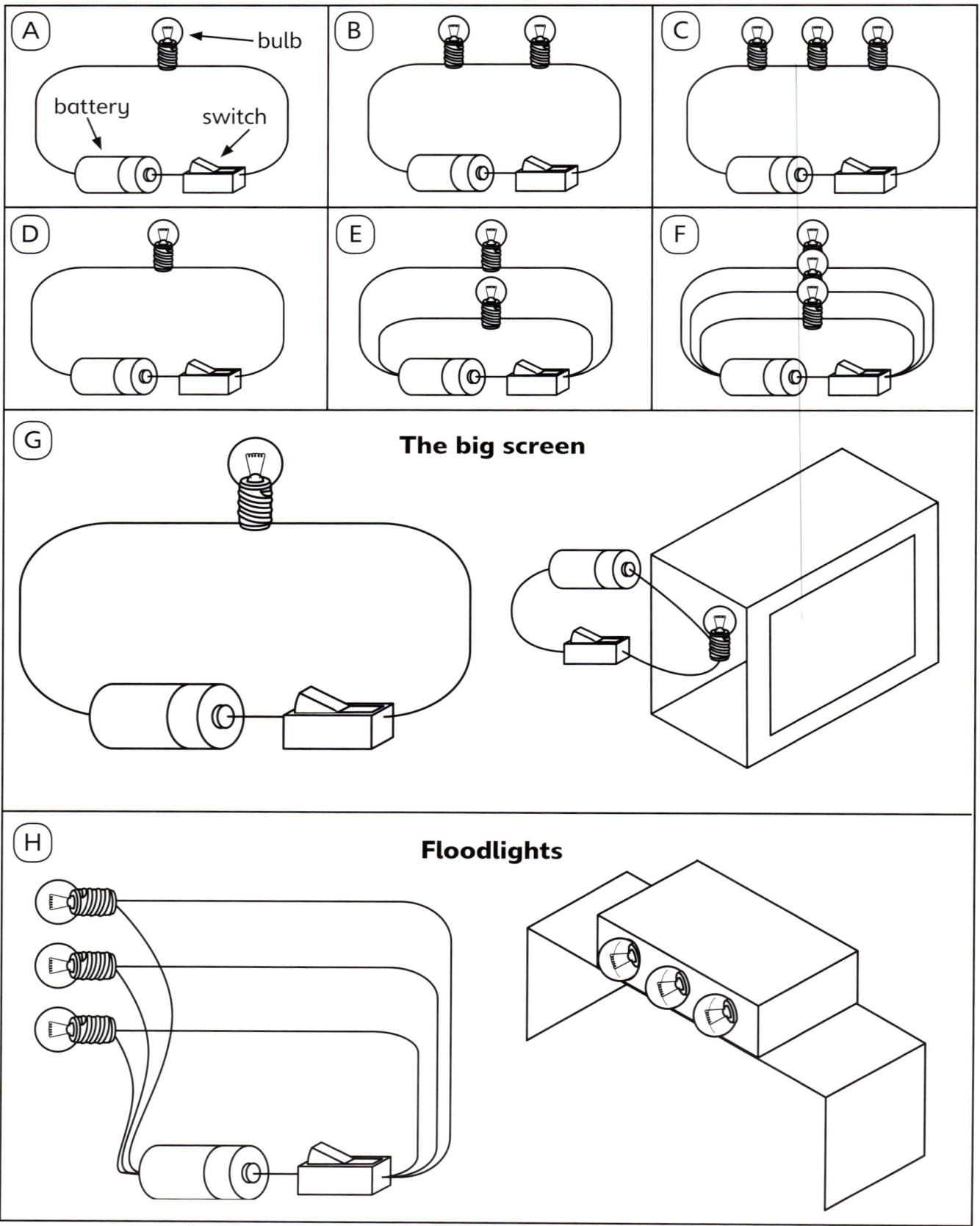

Theme 3 Lesson 3: Finding your way to the ground

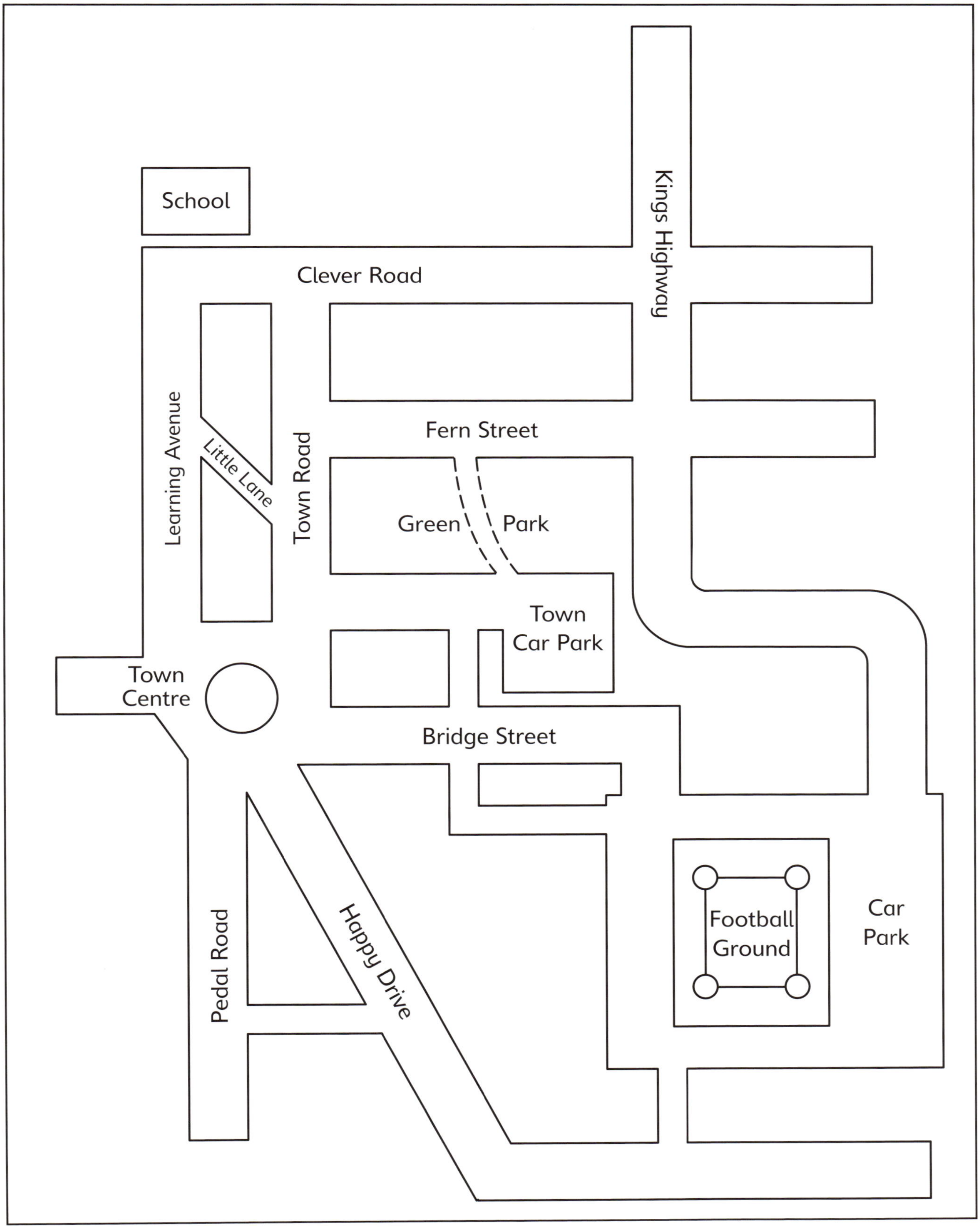

Who's who in football?

BACKGROUND

When children think about a football club they tend to focus on the players but there are many people who help to make the game happen and keep spectators safe. You might want to use this theme to support links with PSHE and citizenship, for example teaching pupils about the range of jobs carried out by people they know and helping them understand how they can develop skills to make their own contribution in the future. In Lesson 3, you could consider, research, discuss and debate topical issues, problems and events and resolve differences by looking at alternatives, making decisions and explaining choices.

You might like to look at the websites of local clubs – there is usually a section on backroom staff. Some of the people have different job titles. Each club is run by a board of directors. These are usually successful local business people who have invested money in the club. They make plans for the future of the club based on the team's performance.

The accounts provided for the fictitious club Brill Town United are extremely simplified. Their purpose is to get children debating issues about how to make the club financially sound. You might like to talk about travel and accommodation costs incurred by the team on away games and perhaps how the stadium could be used for other events.

THE CONTENTS
Lesson 1 (Ages 5–7)
The team behind the team
The children learn the names of the jobs of the backroom staff and what each member of staff does. They can colour in and cut out the model players on page 21 and place them in the model football ground.

Lesson 2 (Ages 7–9)
Backroom staff
The children role-play going to a football match and meeting some people who work for the club before they take their seat. They learn about the backroom staff, make a book about them and create mimes for each job.

Lesson 3 (Ages 9–11)
Running a club
The children learn about the people who work in football besides the players and study a simple weekly balance sheet of a fictitious club. They discover that it is losing money and take on the roles of board directors to come up with a solution for making the club financially sound.

Notes on photocopiables
The team behind the team (page 37)
This sheet features pictures of ten members of backroom staff to cut out and colour in.

Backroom staff (page 38)
This sheet features the job titles and brief job descriptions of all the backroom staff shown on page 37. You can share the information with children or give it to them to help them make a book about backroom staff.

Running a club (page 39)
This page features a weekly balance sheet for a fictitious football club. It offers opportunities for children to practise calculation skills as well as to debate financial issues related to football.

Lesson 1 — The team behind the team

Resources and preparation
- You will need: the model football ground from Theme 3, Lesson 1, the players from Theme 2, Lesson 1, a cardboard cut-out manager, coach and physiotherapist from photocopiable page 37 'The team behind the team'.
- Each child will need: page 37 photocopied onto card, coloured pencils, scissors.
- For the extension activity you will need: two pieces of turf, two plastic trays, a hand fork, a watering can, a measuring cylinder.

What to do
- Gather the children around their model football ground and ask some of them to put one team of players on the pitch. Ask the children who else works at the club besides the players. If some of the children have been to a match they may mention people they have seen such as programme sellers, snack bar assistants, security guards and the manager.
- Tell the children that when the players come out onto the pitch, they are followed by some more people. Stand the cut-out figures of the manager, coach and physiotherapist by the dugout. Ask the children who they are – it doesn't matter if they answer correctly or not at this stage.
- Let the children sit down and hand out copies of photocopiable page 37. Look at the pictures of backroom staff and ask the children how many are wearing tracksuits. They can colour in the tracksuits in the club colours. They may colour in the clothes worn by other staff as they wish.
- Tell the children to cut out the cards and show them how to bend the tabs so that the people stand up. Ask the children to look at the people you put in the dugout and pick the same three from their collection.
- Ask the children to hold up their cards numbered 1, 2 and 3 in turn as you read out the information about them from page 38. Ask the children what they can remember.
- Repeat with three or four of the other people until you have talked about the whole of the team behind the team.
- Tell the children that these people are known as the backroom staff. Ask them which member of the backroom staff they would like to be and why.

Extension
Explain that on a wet day you will often see the groundsman forking the pitch. Ask the children why this is done (to let the water drain away). Show them two pieces of turf and ask them how they could test their idea. One idea would be to put the pieces of turf in trays. Prod one with a hand fork and leave the other untouched, then pour the same amount of water on them from a watering can. Collect the water from the trays in a measuring cylinder to compare how much water drained away from each.

AGES 5–7

Objectives
- To learn about the backroom staff who support the team.
- To talk about what they know.
- To plan and take part in a scientific investigation.

Subject references

English
- Speak with clear diction and appropriate intonation. (NC: KS1 En1 1a)
- Sustain concentration. (NC: KS1 En1 2a)
- Remember specific points that interest them. (NC: KS1 En1 2b)
- Take turns in speaking. (NC: KS1 En1 3a)
- Listen to adults giving detailed explanations. (NC: KS1 En1 9b)

Design and technology
- Cut and shape a range of materials. (NC: KS1 2c)

Science
- Recognise when a test or comparison is unfair. (NC: KS1 Sc1 2d)
- Record observations and measurements. (NC: KS1 Sc1 2f)
- Make simple comparisons. (NC: KS1 Sc1 2h)

Mathematics
- Measures: use simple measuring instruments, reading scale to nearest labelled division. (NC: KS1 Ma3 4c)

Lesson 2 Backroom staff

AGES 7–9

Objectives
- To learn the job titles of the backroom staff at a football club.
- To learn about the jobs of the different members of backroom staff at a football club.
- To make a book about the backroom staff at a football club.

Subject references

English
- Use different ways to help the group move forward, including summarising the main points, reviewing what has been said, clarifying, drawing others in, reaching agreement, considering alternatives and anticipating consequences. (NC: KS2 En1 3f)
- Create, adapt and sustain different roles individually or in groups. (NC: KS2 En1 4a)
- Identify the use and effect of specialist vocabulary. (NC: KS2 En2 5a)

Design and technology
- Generate ideas for products after thinking about who will use them and what they will be used for. (NC: KS2 1a)
- Select appropriate tools and techniques for making their product. (NC: KS2 2a)

Resources and preparation
- For the starter, you may need items for role play: football scarves, old football programmes, yellow jackets for security guards, tickets, a table to serve as a turnstile, a table with empty food packets to serve as a snack bar.
- Each child will need: copies of pages 37 'The team behind the team' and 38 'Backroom staff', paper, glue.
- For the plenary, you will need the following clothes/props for role play: manager - smart blazer or jacket; coach – tracksuit; goalkeeping coach – tracksuit, gloves, ball; physiotherapist – bag; kit manager - pile of clothes; groundsman – anorak and cap; doctor – stethoscope, white coat; development coach – tracksuit, football; match analyst – laptop; performance nutritionist – selection of foods.

Starter
- Some of the children may have been to a football match at a league club. Ask them to tell the class about who they saw while they were there, for example, programme sellers, security guards, turnstile attendants, snack bar workers. The idea is to show that there are more people involved with a club than just the players.
- You could make this into a short play with children taking the roles of club staff and supporters - buying programmes, being checked by security, showing their tickets and buying a snack.

What to do
- Tell the children that there are even more people who work at the football club besides the players. These people are known as the backroom staff. Hand out copies of page 37. Ask the children if they can identify any of the people. They may point out the manager, the coach and the groundsman.
- Give them copies of page 38 and ask them to read about each person in turn, then match the descriptions to the pictures on page 37. Ask them to write the number of the matching picture in the box next to the text.
- When they have finished, check and correct their answers as necessary.
- After the text and pictures have been correctly matched, the children can cut them out and place each picture with its text.
- Tell the children that they are going to make a book about the backroom staff. Ask them for suggestions about how to do this and discuss the pros and cons of each option. Let the children stick down their pictures and text to compile their books.

Differentiation

- Less confident learners could stick each picture on a piece of paper with the appropriate text, then stick the pages together to make a book. They could design and make a front cover.
- More confident learners might like to redraw and colour each picture on a separate page and write or stick the text underneath. Most of the staff could be shown on a training pitch but the doctor could be in a surgery, the kit manager in the changing rooms, the match analyst in an office and the nutritionist preparing a meal.

Assessment

The children can be assessed on the quality of their books. They could be assessed on how well they work together in groups during the plenary.

Plenary

Working in pairs or small groups, the children choose or are given a person to consider. They discuss what actions they could mime to represent this person then one of them performs the mime to the class. All the children present their mimes in turn. They may use props, as suggested in the resources section.

Outcomes

- The children learn the job titles of the backroom staff at a football club.
- They learn about the jobs of the different members of the backroom staff at a football club.
- They make a book about the backroom staff at a football club.

Did you know?

Fred Everiss managed West Bromwich Albion for 46 years – the longest serving Football League manager.

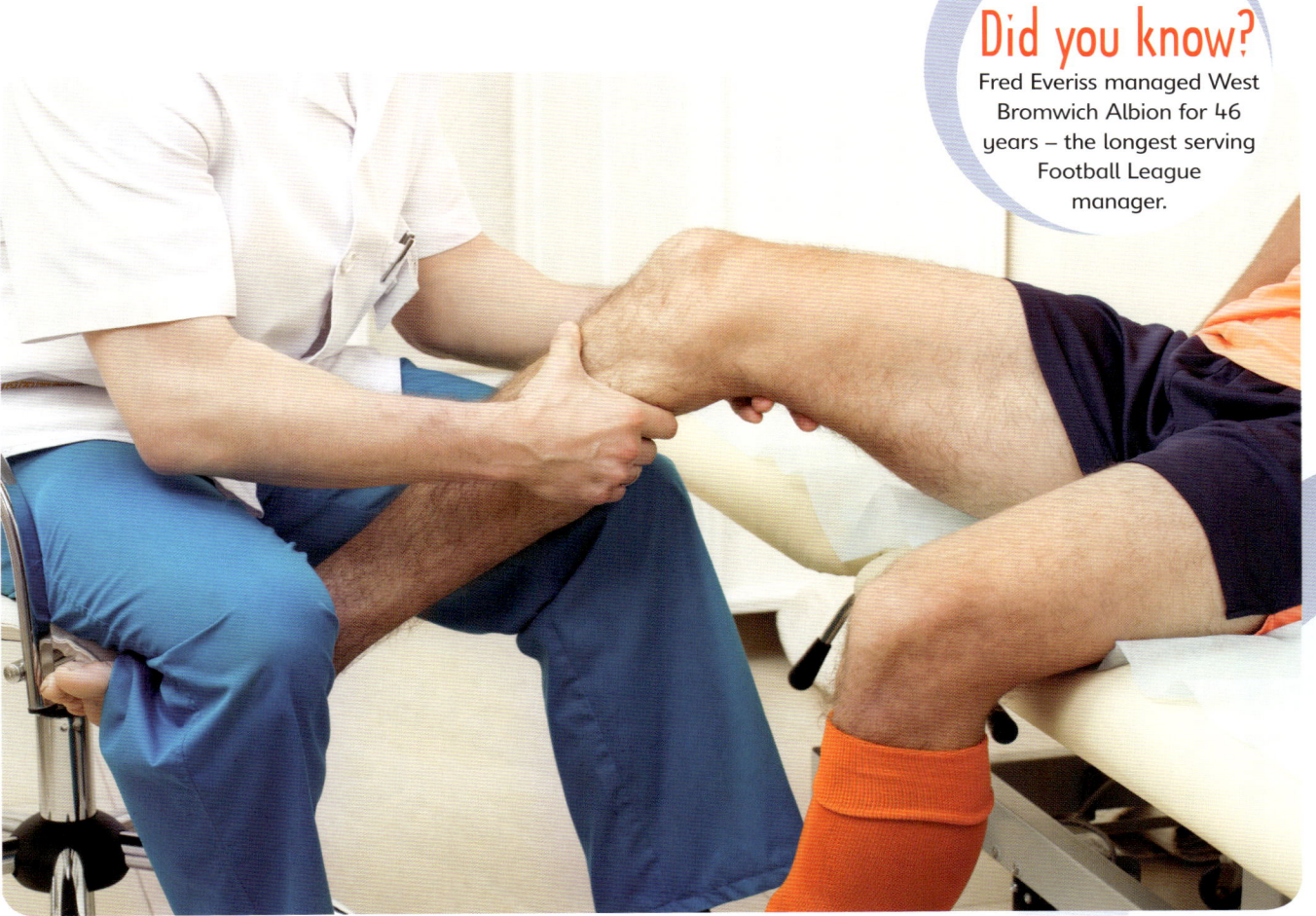

Lesson 3: Running a club

AGES 9–11

Objectives
- To understand some of the finances involved in running a football club.
- To make calculations.
- To take part in a debate and reach a conclusion.
- To write a persuasive letter.

Subject references

English
- Make contributions relevant to the topic and take turns in discussion. (NC: KS2 En1 3a)
- Vary contributions to suit the activity and purpose, including exploratory and tentative comments where ideas are being collected together, and reasoned, evaluative comments as discussion moves to conclusions and actions. (NC: KS2 En1 3b)
- Deal politely with opposing points of view and enable discussion to move on. (NC: KS2 En1 3d)
- Write to persuade, focusing on how arguments and evidence are built up and language used to convince the reader. (NC: KS2 En3 9c)

Mathematics
- Select and use data handling skills when solving problems in other areas of the curriculum. (NC: KS2 Ma4 1a)
- Identify the data necessary to solve a given problem. (NC: KS2 Ma4 1c)

Resources and preparation
Each child will need copies of pages 37, 38 and 39 and access to football programmes.

What to do
- Ask the children to think of club employees they might come across as they arrive at the ground and take their seat. They should mention programme sellers, ticket attendants, shop attendants, snack bar workers and security guards.
- Now ask them who they see as the teams come out onto the pitch. They should mention the players and some of the backroom staff. At this point, you may like to hand out copies of pages 37 and 38 and let the children match the pictures to the descriptions to help them realise that there are more people working for the club than just players.
- Hand out copies of page 39 and explain that this shows the weekly balance sheet of a fictitious football club called Brill Town United. Ask the children to calculate the money taken from ticket sales and add that to all the other income for the week (£221,000) and then total up the expenses for the week (£230,000).
- Ask the children what will happen if the club keeps spending more money than it earns. Look for an answer about it going out of business.
- Tell the children that the club is run by a board of directors. They are usually business people who give the club extra money when it is needed but explain that this is not possible at Brill Town Utd. Arrange the class into groups of directors and ask them how they would solve the club's problems and make the income balance the expenditure.
- Give the groups 20 minutes to come up with a plan and take it in turns to present it to the rest of the class.

Extension
As a consequence of the 'board meeting', it may be felt that extra sponsorship or advertising is needed. The children could write a letter to prospective clients pointing out the advantages of advertising at the ground or sponsoring the club. The children could look at football programmes to see how advertisers and sponsors use a football club. The children could head their letters with a football badge of their own design (see page 20).

Theme 4
Lesson 1: The team behind the team

HOT TOPICS Football

37

Theme 4, Lesson 2: Backroom staff

Manager ☐
Decides who plays for the club.
Plans the training.
Picks the team.
Encourages the team before the game.

Coach ☐
Runs the training sessions.
Checks fitness of players in training.
Follows manager's training plan.

Goalkeeping coach ☐
Runs training sessions for goalkeepers.
Checks fitness of goalkeepers.
Brings in other players for a goal scoring competition.

Physiotherapist ☐
Checks fitness of players before a game.
Helps with injuries on the pitch.
Helps players recover from injuries after a game.

Kit manager ☐
Makes sure each player has clean kit for matches.
Makes sure all dirty kit is cleaned.

Groundsman ☐
Cuts the grass.
Marks out the pitch.
Makes sure the surface is safe to play on.

Doctor ☐
Treats ill players.
Treats injured players.
Works with physiotherapist.

Development coach ☐
Assesses young players.
Sets up a youth team.
Helps youth team players become first-team players.

Match analyst ☐
Uses computer to analyse how players play.
Helps attackers see how they attack.
Helps defenders see how they defend.
Helps midfielders see how they play.

Performance nutritionist ☐
Prepares diets for energy in games.
Prepares diets to help injured players recover quickly.
Prepares diets to keep players healthy.

Theme 4 Lesson 3: Running a club

Brill Town United's weekly balance sheet

Income for the week

Money from ticket sales	
8,000 adult tickets at £20	_____
4,000 concession tickets at £10	_____
Profit from shop	2,000
Money from sponsors	4,000
Profit from selling food and drink	3,000
Profit from selling programmes	2,000
Money from advertising	10,000
Total income for the week	£_____

Expenditure for the week

Wages

Players	180,000
Backroom staff	40,000
Ticket office staff	1,000
Catering staff	500
Shop staff	500
Security staff	2,000
General office staff	2,000
Electricity, rates and other expenses	4,000
Total expenditure for the week	£_____

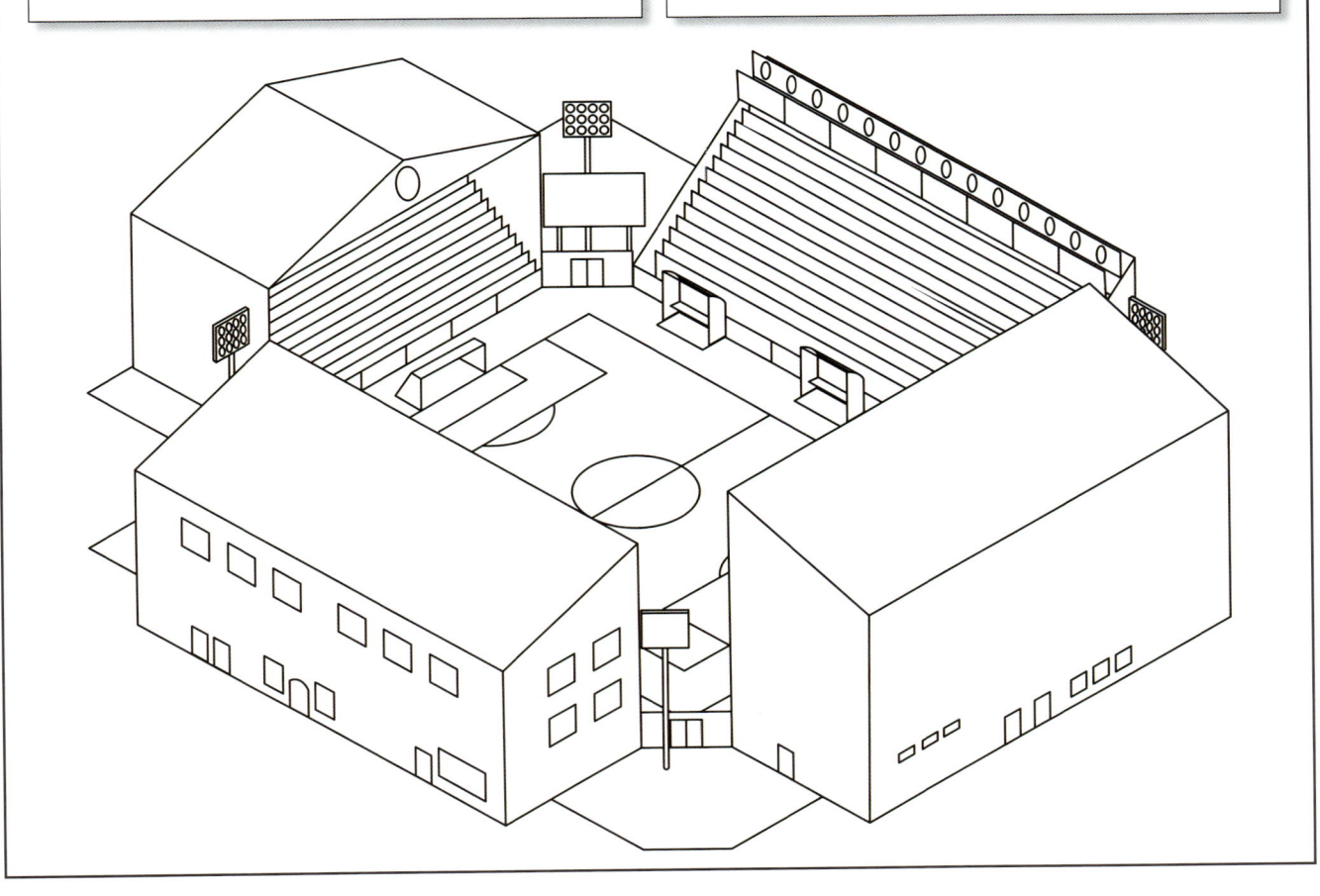

HOT TOPICS Football

Theme 5: Football players

BACKGROUND

There are many ways to describe team positions on the field. One format was developed by Preston North End in 1888. It was used widely by clubs for many years, and is shown in the diagram below. It is not often used now but children reading about players in the past may come across terms such as inside right, half back or centre half so they may find this information helpful.

Team formations have changed since those days and there are more general names for positions, as shown in the table on page 46. The full backs are now centre backs and they each have a wing back next to them. This is known as the back line. The half backs are now called midfielders and there may be four of them with one known as the midfield engine or play-maker who organises attacks. The two midfielders on the wings may be like old-style wingers. The striker (and there may be two) occupies the area of the old centre and inside forwards.

This website gives details of more modern positions and their roles: http://news.bbc.co.uk/sport1/hi/football/rules_and_equipment/4197420.stm

THE CONTENTS

Lesson 1 (Ages 5–7)
Basic skills
The children learn to identify nine basic football skills. They work out a skills practice programme and try it out.

Lesson 2 (Ages 7–9)
The skills in a team
The children learn about nine basic football skills, try some of them, then relate the skills to positions in the team. They examine the skills of the goalkeeper and some of the children try them out.

Lesson 3 (Ages 9–11)
Meeting a player
The children study a questionnaire, think of additional questions of their own, and email them to a football club. They interview one or more players and afterwards reflect on the life of a footballer.

Notes on photocopiables

Basic skills (page 45)
This page has pictures of nine different football skills with a block of corresponding labels. The children cut out the pictures and labels, match them up, then stick them to separate cards to use in making up a skills development programme. Answers: 1) lofting a pass; 2) trapping the ball; 3) volley shot; 4) back pass; 5) running with the ball; 6) dribbling; 7) heading; 8) pass with inside of foot; 9) shooting.

The skills in a team (page 46)
A table relates the positions in the team to the skills needed to play each position well. A series of pictures shows the skills needed by a goalkeeper.

Meeting a player (page 47)
This page lists 18 questions that children might ask a player in an interview.

Lesson 1 Basic skills

Resources and preparation
- Each child will need: a copy of page 45 'Basic skills', scissors, coloured pencils, glue, nine green cards.
- Each group will need: a large sheet of card, some Blu-Tack®, a football. The children will need access to four cones set up for dribbling, a wall or goal nets for shooting practice.
- You will need plenty of helpers to supervise the children's training programme.

What to do
- Tell the children that they are going to learn about different football skills. Hand out copies of page 45 and ask them to cut out the players and labels.
- Ask the children to work in groups to match the pictures to the labels then check their answers.
- Let the children colour in the players' kit in the colours of their favourite team.
- Give each child nine green cards and ask them to stick a picture on each with the correct label underneath. Check that they have placed the labels correctly before they glue them on.
- Tell the children that they each have nine skills cards that they are going to use to plan some skills practice. Remind them that football is a team game so they can begin by working in pairs to practise passing with the inside of the foot and trapping the ball (for children who have not played much football before) or lofting passes and stopping them with a raised foot (for those who play regularly).
- The children could compare passing the ball with the inside of the foot and with the toe. They should find that they have more control when passing with the inside of the foot.
- Tell the children that some skills, such as running with the ball, can be practised on their own. Set up some cones to dribble round and let them shoot against a wall or into a goal net.

Extension
- Let the children work in pairs or groups of three or four and use their cards to set out a plan for their own skills practice programme. They could stick the cards with Blu-Tack® onto a larger sheet to make a temporary skills development programme and show it to the rest of the class.
- Provide opportunities for children to regularly try out their training programmes throughout your teaching of football-based topics.

AGES 5–7

Objectives
- To identify a range of football skills.
- To plan a programme to develop skills.
- To take part in a practice programme to develop football skills.

Subject references

English
- Take turns in speaking. (NC: KS1 En1 3a)
- Take different views into account. (NC: KS1 En1 3c)
- Use adventurous and wide-ranging vocabulary. (NC: KS1 En3 1a)

Physical education
- Explore basic skills, actions and ideas with increasing understanding. (NC: KS1 1a)
- Remember and repeat simple skills and actions with increasing control and coordination. (NC: KS1 1b)
- Explore how to choose and apply skills and actions in sequence and in combination. (NC: KS1 2a)
- Vary the way they perform skills by using simple tactics and movement phrases. (NC: KS1 2b)
- Describe what they have done. (NC: KS1 3a)
- Observe, describe and copy what others have done. (NC: KS1 3b)
- Use what they have learned to improve the quality and control of their work. (NC: KS1 3c)
- Travel with, send and receive a ball in different ways. (NC: KS1 7a)
- Develop these skills for simple net, striking/fielding and invasion-type games. (NC: KS1 7b)

Lesson 2   The skills in a team

AGES 7–9

Objectives
- To identify a range of football skills.
- To try some of the football skills.
- To match the skills to positions in the team.
- To match their developing skills against a position in the team.
- To study the skills of the goalkeeper.

Subject references

Physical education
- Consolidate their existing skills and gain new ones. (NC: KS2 1a)
- Perform actions and skills with more consistent control and quality. (NC: KS2 1b)
- Identify what makes a performance more effective. (NC: KS2 3a)
- Suggest improvements based on this information. (NC: KS2 3b)

English
- Qualify and justify what they think after listening to others' questions or accounts. (NC: KS2 En1 3c)
- Broaden their vocabulary and use it in inventive ways. (NC: KS2 En3 1b)

Resources and preparation
- For the starter, each child will need: a copy of page 45 'Basic skills', coloured pencils, scissors, glue and a blank sheet of paper.
- You will need: access to the school field or hall, cones, footballs, helpers to supervise the activities.
- For the main activity, each child will need: a copy of page 46 'The skills in a team'.

Starter
- Ask the children what football skills they know. Prompt them to talk about shooting, passing or tackling.
- Hand out copies of page 45 and let the children colour in the players in any colours they like, then ask them to cut them out, cut out the labels and match them up. Stick the pictures with their matching labels on a sheet of paper headed 'Football skills to practise'.
- Let the children work in pairs to practise passing and trapping the ball. They can work on their own to practise running with the ball and dribbling through cones.

What to do
- Tell the children that they have been practising the skills of an outfield player and ask them if they know the names of any of the outfield positions (defender, full back, centre back, wing back, midfielder and striker).
- If the class has made a model football ground with a pitch and a set of players you might ask a few children in turn to position players where they think they line up at the beginning of a game. Defenders and backs stand near the goals, midfielders and wingers are in the middle third of their half and strikers stand in the third nearest the half-way line.
- Remind the children about the skills they have just performed and ask them what skills they think each player should have. For example, a striker should be good at shooting and a defender should be a good header.
- Hand out copies of page 46 and let the children check their ideas against the answers in the table.
- Point out that tackling is mentioned as a skill in the table. Look for an answer about taking the ball away from the other player. Say that this is a tricky skill to accomplish and players must take extra care to avoid injury to their opponent and themselves.
- Let the children discuss their own skills (with the exception of tackling) in pairs or small groups and decide which position their skills may be best suited to. See if you can create one or more class teams with defenders, midfielders and strikers.
- Tell the children that there is one player they have not studied yet – the goalkeeper. Look at the pictures on photocopiable page 46 and get the whole class to adopt the goalkeeper stance. Talk them through the remaining pictures and ask if anyone wants to try some goalkeeping skills. If one or two

42

children volunteer, let the rest of the class in turn send in some shots for them to save, punch or throw out.

Differentiation
- Less confident learners may need help in matching the labels to the actions on page 45.
- More confident learners might like to assess how good they could be as a football coach or manager from their knowledge of matching skills to positions on page 46.

Assessment
The children can be assessed on matching skills to pictures, knowledge of the positions on the field and matching skills to positions.

Plenary
The children could work out a programme for practising their skills with their friends and try it out over the following days.

Outcomes
- The children can identify a range of football skills.
- They can plan a programme to develop skills.
- They can take part in a practice programme to develop football skills.

Lesson 3 — Meeting a player

AGES 9–11

Objectives
- To find out about the life of a footballer.
- To ask questions politely.

Subject references

English
- Speak audibly and clearly, using spoken standard English in formal contexts. (NC: KS2 En1 1e)
- Listen to live talks. (NC: KS2 En1 9a)
- Identify the gist of an account and evaluate what they hear. (NC: KS2 En1 2a)
- Ask relevant questions to clarify, extend and follow up ideas. (NC: KS2 En1 2b)
- Develop writing by planning and drafting. (NC: KS2 En3 2a–f)

ICT
- Learn how to develop and refine ideas by bringing together text, tables, images and sound as appropriate. (NC: KS2 2a)
- Learn how to share and exchange information in a variety of forms including email. (NC: KS2 3a)

Did you know?
Substitutes were introduced into the Football League in the 1965-66 season.

Resources and preparation
- You will need to contact a football club well in advance of the lesson, inviting one or more players to visit your class. You could send a copy of page 47 'Meeting a player' with your request to give the footballer an idea of the questions that they would be asked. Later, you could send more questions devised by the children.
- Make sure that office staff and colleagues at school are aware of the planned visit and arrange to offer your visitor some form of hospitality before the interview. You will need a room in a quiet part of the school for the visit and the class should not be disturbed while the interview is taking place.
- Before the interview, allocate questions to the children by cutting them out from a copy of page 47 or let them write out or type up their own. Mark on a master copy who has been given each question so that you can prompt the children during the interview.

What to do
- If you are successful in arranging a visit, tell the children about it and say that they will have the chance to interview the player. If not, you could ask a parent who has played or coached or even consider taking on the role yourself, either as a fictional or a famous player.
- Hand out copies of page 47 and say that you have already sent these questions to the football club but they can add more of their own. Go through the questions with the children and ask them what else they would like to know. If the club has told you who will be attending, the children may have more specific but non-intrusive questions to ask such as 'How did you feel when you held up the cup?' or 'Who was your favourite player when you were young and why?'
- When they have agreed on all the questions, the children can set them out in a second questionnaire and use ICT to design it. Compare the designs and presentations and let the children decide which one to send.
- The child whose design is selected could email the questionnaire to the club with an accompanying letter written by the class.

Extension
- Distribute the questions to the children before the footballer arrives.
- Welcome and introduce the player or players and explain how the interview will be conducted.
- During the interview, the children should try to remember the response to their question but you may find it useful to make notes on the master copy.
- At the end of the interview, ask the player if they would like to add anything, then bring the interview to a close by letting one or more children give a vote of thanks.

Theme 5
Lesson 1 Basic skills

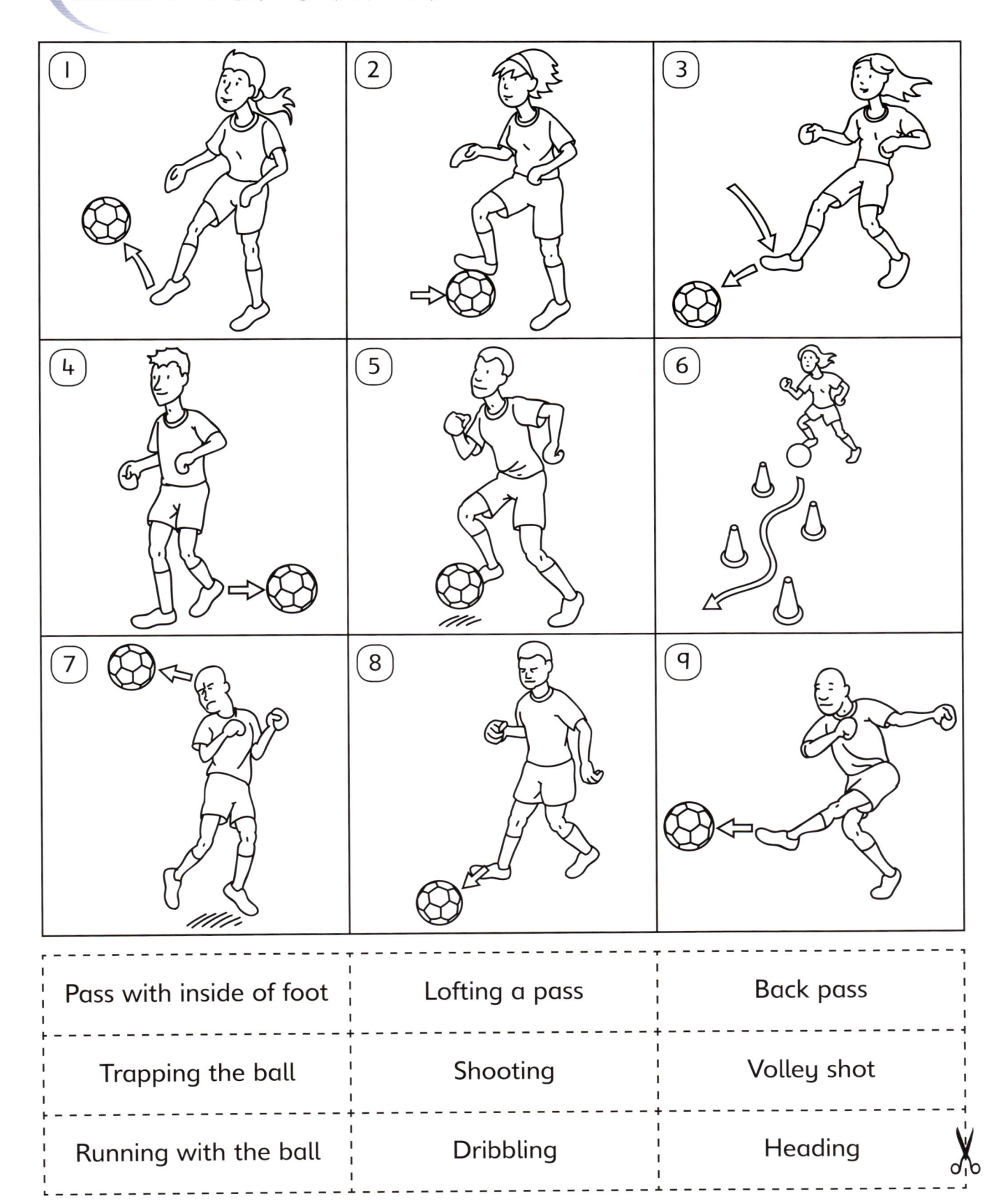

Pass with inside of foot	Lofting a pass	Back pass
Trapping the ball	Shooting	Volley shot
Running with the ball	Dribbling	Heading

HOT TOPICS Football

45

Theme 5 Lesson 2: The skills in a team

Position	Tackling	Heading	Passing	Speed and running with the ball	Dribbling	Shooting
Full/wing back	✓	✓	✓	✓		
Centre back	✓	✓	✓			
Midfielder	✓		✓	✓		
Winger			✓	✓	✓	✓
Striker		✓		✓	✓	✓

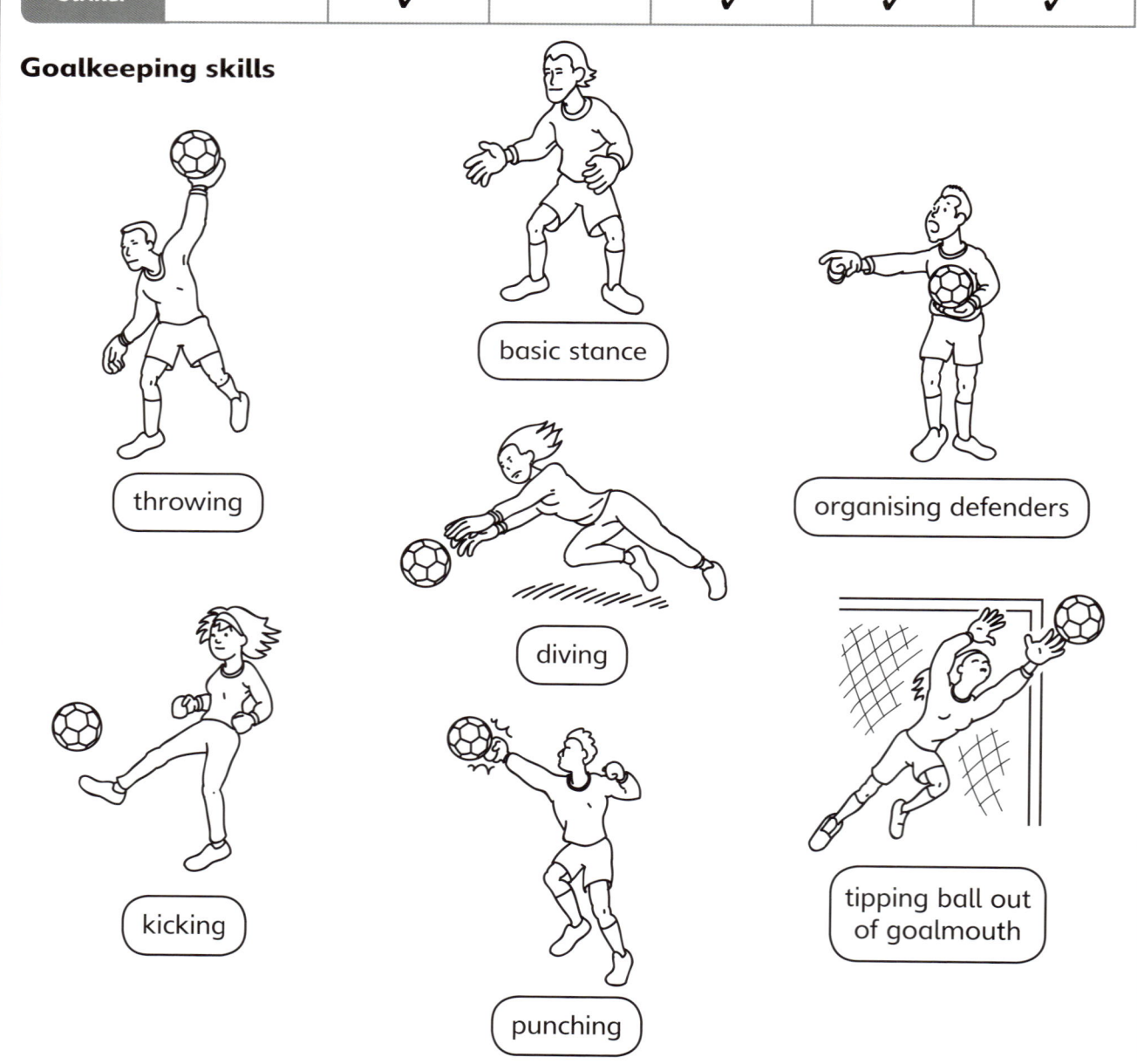

Goalkeeping skills

- throwing
- basic stance
- organising defenders
- diving
- kicking
- punching
- tipping ball out of goalmouth

Theme 5 Lesson 3 — Meeting a player

List of questions to copy and send to interviewee/for children to ask.

1 Which sports did you play when you were growing up?

2 Who were the first team you ever played for and how old were you when you played for them?

3 Were any other people in your family good at football or other sports?

4 How did your football career develop from playing for that team to joining your first professional club?

5 Who were the people who helped you on your way?

6 How did you feel when you joined your current club?

7 Have there been times when you felt your career was not going well? If so, how did you stay motivated?

8 What early success are you most proud of?

9 What is your training schedule during the week?

10 What do you like best about training?

11 What do you like least about training?

12 What do you do to relax?

13 How does being a footballer affect what you can eat?

14 How do you prepare for the game on match day?

15 How do you feel when the team wins?

16 How do you motivate yourself when the team loses?

17 Footballers often look serious when they are interviewed after the match, even if their team has won. Is there a place for a sense of humour in sport? If there is, when is it useful?

18 What advice would you give to budding footballers?

HOT TOPICS Football

Theme 6

The game

BACKGROUND

When football was being established during the 19th century it was considered a sport for gentlemen, even though in the past mob football could be played by anyone and had no rules. In the first rules of football there was no mention of fouls or penalties as it was not considered to be fair play.

When teams met for a match each one brought an umpire who made sure that the game took place in an orderly way as set out by the rules. When a timekeeper was introduced he also became the person to whom the umpires referred if there was a dispute and in time he became known as the referee. He stayed on the field of play to supervise the game while the umpires became his assistants and ran the line – the linesmen. Each team now has a dugout where the substitutes sit. The area marked out in front of this is called the technical area in which the manager can move and shout instructions. The fourth official is now the timekeeper and also supervises the behaviour of the people in the dugouts as well as substitutions. The fourth official can take over as referee or assistant referee in an emergency. A map showing the paths taken by the officials during a game can be found at: www.watchandwhistle.org/watchpix/PPT_DIG.GIF

A good commentator, especially on radio, describes the action in detail using football terms such as 'throw-in' and 'free kick' which the children might like to add to the commentaries they will devise in Lesson 2. An indirect free kick is the most usual type of free kick given. A player cannot score a goal from an indirect free kick - they must pass to another player. A direct free kick may be given close to goal outside the penalty box for a serious foul and the player can shoot straight at goal to try and score. More information about the rules and many other aspects of the game can be found at: news.bbc.co.uk/sport1/hi/football/rules_and_equipment/default.stm

Everyone who follows football has an opinion on what the manager should be doing and in Lesson 3 some simple scenarios are provided to let the children think about what it would be like to manage a group of players.

THE CONTENTS

Lesson 1 (Ages 5–7)
Match officials
The children learn about the uniform and equipment used by the match officials. They learn about the signals made by the referee and assistant referee and the positions of officials on the field.

Lesson 2 (Ages 7–9)
Football commentary
The children learn to identify different football skills. They write captions for the actions illustrated on photocopiable page 54 and read them in sequence to make a football commentary.

Lesson 3 (Ages 9–11)
Team selection
The children rate their own football skills then study information about players' skill ratings at a fictitious football club. They imagine they are the manager and use this information to pick a goalkeeper, centre backs, midfielders and strikers for a game and deal with issues about the players' performances.

Notes on photocopiables

Match officials: signals (page 53)
This sheet features some of the signals made by the referee and the assistant referees.

Football commentary (page 54)
Six pictures provide snapshots of action from a match. Each picture needs a caption which can be read out as a commentary.

Team selection (page 55)
This page provides the training performance ratings for fictitious players for the children to use to select a team. (Answers: 1 Casey; 2 Dale and Drew; 3 Franky and Jamila; 4 Jamie and Shiola.)

Lesson 1 — Match officials

Resources and preparation
- You will need: three pairs of black shorts, three black shirts, a whistle, 15 yellow flags (one per pair of children).
- Each child will need: a copy of page 53 'Match officials: signals'.
- Make copies of page 21 and cut the players into groups of three for the children to colour as match officials.
- Each group of three will need: scissors, glue, a piece of yellow card, black pencils or crayons.

What to do
- Arrange for three children to leave the classroom and dress up in black shirts and shorts. Give one child a whistle and the other two a yellow flag each. Ask them to wait outside the door while you tell the class that you are going to introduce three more people who are also present at a football game. Call the children back in and ask the class who they are. (The referee and assistant referees who are also known as linesmen or lineswomen.)
- Tell the children that the referee blows the whistle to start and stop play; he blows a long note to signal half-time and when the game is over. Let the 'referee' demonstrate.
- The assistant referees use their flags to show the referee, players and spectators how the play should continue or when rules have been broken. Let the 'assistant referees' wave their flags.
- Give everyone a copy of page 53 and explain that they are all going to get a chance to be a referee and an assistant referee. Working in pairs, let the children take turns to give a signal from the sheet while the other tries to guess what it is.
- Select the child who gives the clearest signals to demonstrate to the whole class, while the children try to identify the signals without looking at their sheets.

Extension
- Tell the children that they are going to find out where the officials go on a football pitch, but first they have to make them. Give each group of three the card with three players to cut out and colour in as match officials (black uniforms).
- Tell the children to make two yellow flags from the card and stick them on two of the officials.
- Use the online diagram (see 'Background' page 48) to help the children put their officials on the pitch and move them along the paths they take during a match.

AGES 5–7

Objectives
- To learn how to recognise the match officials.
- To identify the signals made by the referee.
- To identify the signals made by the assistant referee.
- To know the positions of the match officials on the pitch.

Subject references
Physical education
- Use movement imaginatively, responding to stimuli and performing basic skills. (NC: KS1 6a)
- Express and communicate ideas and feelings. (NC: KS1 6d)

English
- Read on sight high-frequency words and other familiar words. (NC: KS1 En2 1e)
- Use the organisational features of non-fiction texts, including captions, to find information. (NC: KS1 En2 2a)

Lesson 2 — Football commentary

AGES 7–9

Objectives
- To perform the basic football skills.
- To identify the use of different skills in a football game.
- To write captions for activities in a football game.
- To read the captions in sequence to make a football commentary.

Subject references

Physical education
- Perform actions and skills with more consistent control and quality. (NC: KS2 1b)

English
- Use vocabulary and syntax that enables them to communicate more complex meanings. (NC: KS2 En1 1a)
- Gain and maintain the interest and response of different audiences. (NC: KS2 En1 1b)
- Plan – note and develop ideas. (NC: KS2 En3 2a)
- Present – prepare a neat, correct and clear final copy. (NC: KS2 En3 2e)
- Inform and explain, focusing on the subject matter and how to convey it in sufficient detail for the reader. (NC: KS2 En3 9b)

Resources and preparation
- For the starter, you will need: access to the school field or hall and a number of helpers to supervise the activity. Set out two or three lines in the following way: a cone at one end where the player receives a pass; a space of several metres where the player runs with the ball; four cones for the player to dribble round; a space of several metres across which the player shoots at a table on its side.
- You will also need: a short television recording of a match with a clear commentary, and the facility to play it back to your class, pausing and rewinding as necessary.
- Each child will need: a copy of page 54 'Football commentary', coloured pencils, scissors, a long strip of card, paper and glue.

Starter
- Tell the children that you have worked out a short training programme and you want them all to take part. Take them to where the cones and table are set up and demonstrate what you want the children to do in turn. (Receive the ball from a pass, run with it, dribble it through the cones and shoot.) Let all the children try the training exercise three times.
- Ask the children to describe what they did then tell them they are going learn how to describe what happens in a football match, just like a commentator.

What to do
- Play back a short recording of a football match. Ask the children to pay particular attention to the commentary. Stop the film, for example, when one player is passing to another or heading the ball towards goal. Point out what the key players in the action are doing (passing and receiving the ball/ heading the ball down while the goalkeeper comes out to make a save).
- Tell the children that they are going to learn to be football commentators by writing captions for six manoeuvres or incidents in a match.
- Give them copies of page 54 and ask them to look at each picture in turn, decide what is happening, then write a caption to describe it. It might help if they colour in the players' kit, showing opposing teams. You may like to talk about the first picture with the class to help them distinguish the action between the players. (The captions could be: 1) Number 7 passes the ball with his right foot to number 11 while the other team's number 9 stands and watches; 2) Number 7 lofts the ball into the air. The other team's number 9 tries to head it but misses; 3) Number 8 chests the ball down and runs with it; 4) Number 5 makes a sliding tackle but misses and number 8 goes on; 5) Number 8 lifts the ball with his right foot to number 7 who jumps to head it while the goalkeeper stands and watches; 6) Number 7 heads past their opponents' number 2 and the goalkeeper to score a goal.)
- When the captions are accurate, let the children cut out the pictures, stick them in sequence on a long piece of card then write out their captions neatly and stick them underneath the pictures.

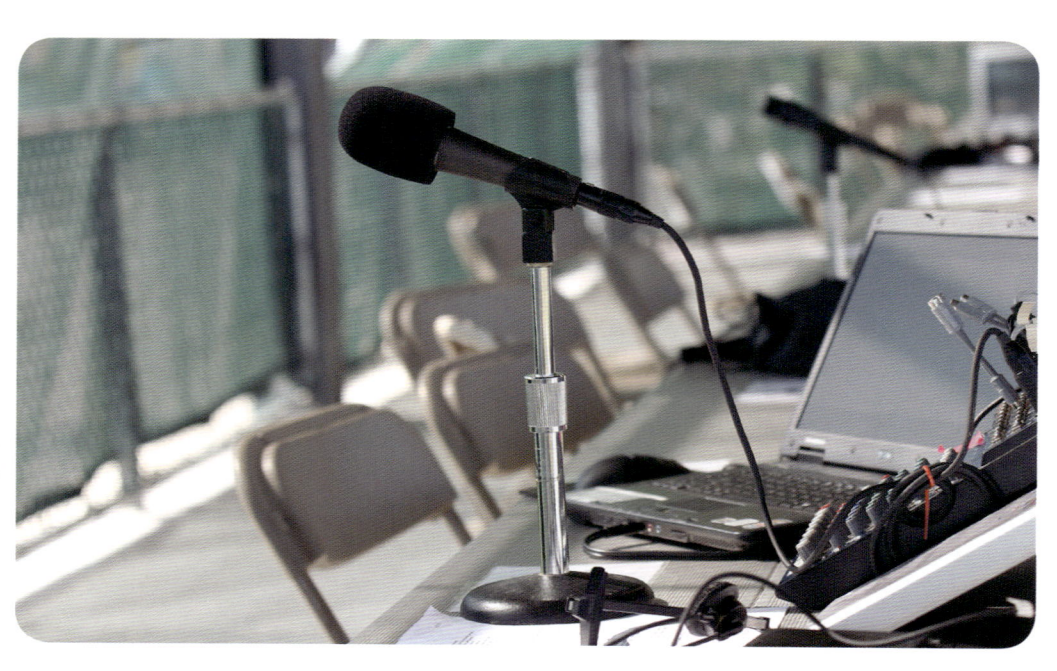

Did you know?
The first football game to be televised live was the 1938 FA Cup final.

Differentiation
- Less confident learners will need help in describing the action in the pictures and writing it down.
- More confident learners could draw their own pictures and add captions, for example, relating how the opposing team fights back to equalise.

Assessment
The children could be assessed on their descriptions of the action in the pictures and on how neatly they write the captions. They could also be assessed on how they read out the captions and make them flow together.

Plenary
You could select several children who have written contrasting accounts to read out their captions in the form of a commentary.

Outcomes
- The children can perform basic football skills.
- They can identify skills being used in a football game.
- They can write captions for action/incidents in a football game.
- They can read the captions in sequence to make a football commentary.

51

Lesson 3 — Team selection

AGES 9–11

Objectives
- To know that equipment can be set up to provide training.
- To know that in training both the players and coach assess performance.
- To know that players' performance in training is used in team selection.
- To know that players are selected for positions in the team on the strength of their abilities.

Subject references

Physical education
- Perform actions and skills with more consistent control and quality. (NC: KS2 1b)
- Identify what makes a performance effective. (NC: KS2 3a)
- Suggest improvements based on this information. (NC: KS2 3b)

Mathematics
- Identify data necessary to solve a given problem. (NC: KS2 Ma4 1c)
- Explain and justify their methods and reasoning. (NC: KS2 Ma4 1h)
- Draw conclusions from statistics. (NC: KS2 Ma4 2f)

English
- Make contributions relevant to the topic and take turns in discussion. (NC: KS2 En1 3a)

Resources and preparation
- You will need: access to the school field or hall and a number of helpers to supervise the activity. Set out two or three lines in the following way: a cone at one end where the player receives a pass; a space of several metres where the player runs with the ball; four cones for the player to dribble round; a space of several metres across which the player shoots at a table on its side.
- Each child will need: a copy of page 55 'Team selection'.

What to do
- Tell the children that you have worked out a short training programme and you want them all to take part. Take them to where the cones and table are set up and demonstrate what you want the children to do in turn. (Receive the ball from a pass, dribble through the cones and shoot.) Let all the children try the training exercise three times.
- Ask each child how well they thought they performed on a scale of 1–10 and what they could do to improve.
- Tell the children that a team has been practising and the coach has written down their scores for the manager to look at. The manager will use the scores to pick the players for the match.
- Hand out copies of page 55. Tell the children that they are the manager of the team and their first task is to pick the goalkeeper. Look at the performance marks with the children and ask them each to write down which goalkeeper they think should play. Ask them each to say who they have chosen and why.
- Go through question 2 from the team selection sheet with the children and ask them each to pick two centre backs. Discuss their decisions. Repeat with questions 3 and 4.

Extension
- Discuss these issues with the children:
1) Tell the children that the match analyst thinks the way to win the next game is for the goalkeeper to make some big goal kicks for the strikers to head into the net. Do they think, as managers, that they should change the goalkeeper? (*Could change to Bobby.*)
2) Drew thinks his rating for speed and running with the ball will make him a good striker. Do the managers agree? (*No, his other striking skills are not high enough.*)
3) The match analyst thinks the next opponents will send a lot of high balls into the midfield for their players to head on to the strikers. Do the managers think they might need to change one of their own midfield players to improve their chances of winning the headers and preventing attacks? (*Replace Franky with Ellis.*)

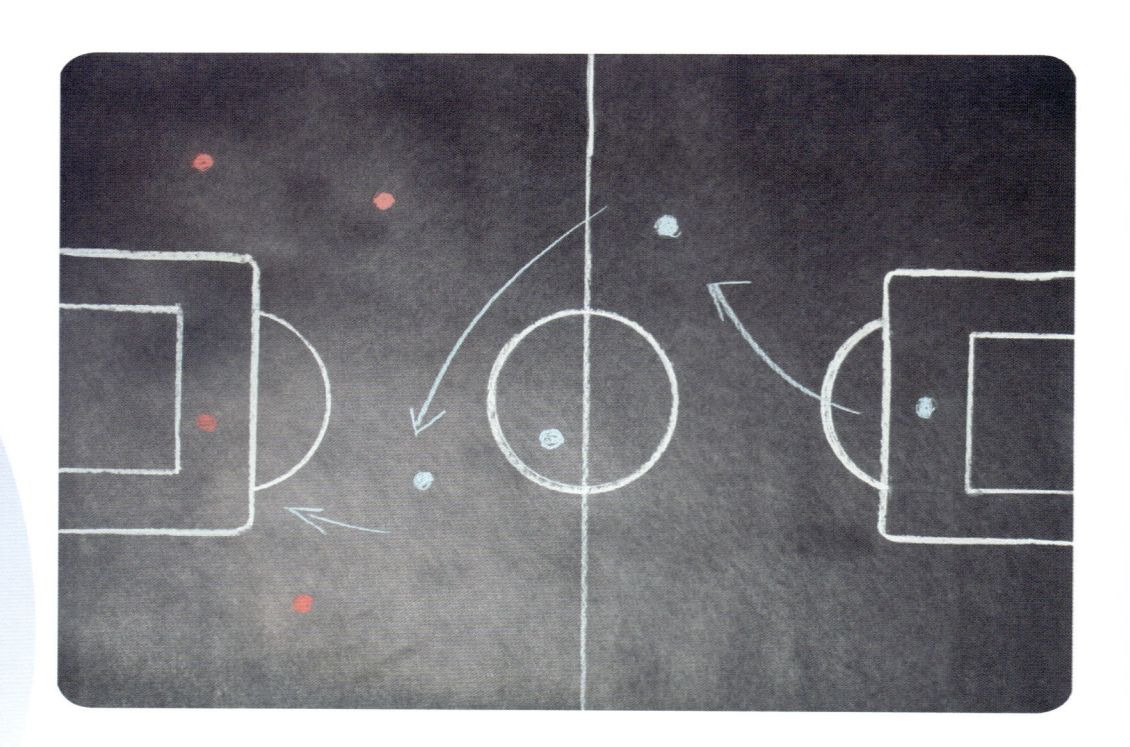

Theme 6, Lesson 1: Match officials: signals

1 Kick-off – referee	2 Corner – referee	3 Goal kick – referee	4 Throw in – referee
5 Penalty – referee points to penalty spot	6 Advantage – referee	7 Indirect free kick – referee	8 Caution – referee (yellow or red card)
9 Offside – assistant referee	10 Corner – assistant referee	11 Goal kick – assistant referee	12 Penalty – assistant referee
13 Throw in (left) – assistant referee	14 Throw in (right) – assistant referee	15 Attention referee! – assistant referee	16 Substitute – assistant referee

HOT TOPICS Football

Football commentary

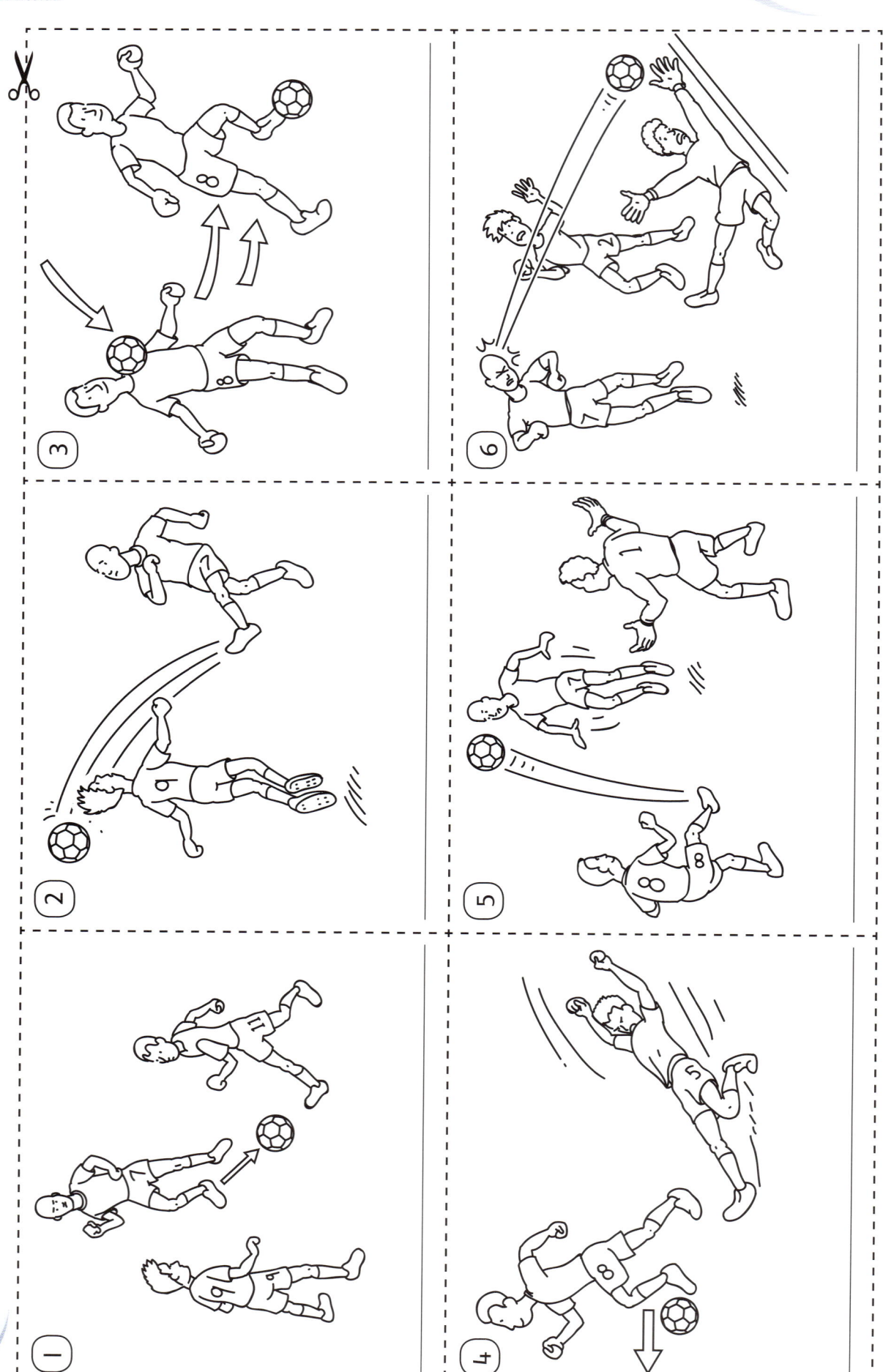

Theme 6 Lesson 2

54

HOT TOPICS Football

Theme 6 Lesson 3: Team selection

Goalkeepers (performance out of 10)

1 Which one would you choose to play? _____

Player	Shot stopping	Catching	Throwing	Kicking	Diving	Punching
Alex	8	9	7	7	8	6
Bobby	7	8	7	9	7	5
Casey	8	9	8	7	8	6

Outfield players (performance out of 10)

2 Ahmed, Dale and Drew are centre backs. They need to be good at tackling, heading and passing. Which two would you pick to play?

_____

3 Ellis, Franky and Jamila are midfielders. They need to be good at tackling, passing and speed and running with the ball. Which two would you pick to play?

_____

4 Jamie, Jesse, Kelly and Shiola are strikers. They need to be good at heading, speed and running with the ball, dribbling and shooting. Which two would you pick to play?

_____

Player	Tackling	Heading	Passing	Speed and running with the ball	Dribbling	Shooting
Ahmed	8	8	7	8	8	7
Dale	9	8	8	7	7	6
Drew	8	9	9	9	7	7
Ellis	8	9	8	8	9	7
Franky	9	7	9	8	8	7
Jamila	8	8	9	8	7	7
Jamie	5	7	5	9	8	9
Jesse	7	9	6	8	7	8
Kelly	8	8	7	8	8	9
Shiola	6	8	7	9	8	9

HOT TOPICS Football

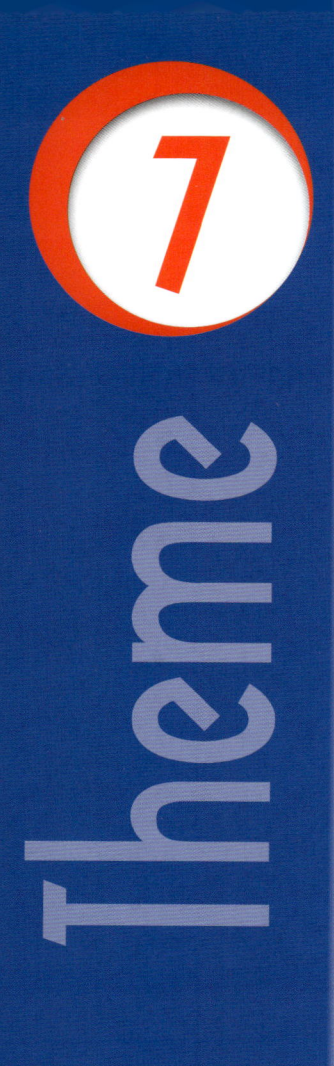

Theme 7: The football season

BACKGROUND
Football teams play in leagues. While the first team may play in the Premiership or Championship, for example, the reserve sides will play in another league with local teams from different, lower divisions.

League tables record the results of matches and show how well a team is performing. They can be used to predict the outcome of future games. The form guide of the last six games, often given in team statistics, shows the run of losses (L), wins (W) and draws (D), for example: LLWDLW. These are used in predictions, too. Predicting results should be considered as part of the enjoyment of football and in discussions should not be linked with any form of gambling.

Towards the end of the season, the positions for automatic promotion places, play-off places (where the teams play in a short knock-out competition – see Theme 9 – to gain promotion) and relegation places are shown by dotted lines or a different tint in the tables published in newspapers, magazines and online.

THE CONTENTS
Lesson 1 (Ages 5–7)
Tables and results
The children study a simple sheet of data about six football teams. They look at their current positions in the table, work out how many goals are scored in the next three games, see how their positions change and how many points the teams get from their games.

Lesson 2 (Ages 7–9)
Studying tables
The children look at part of a football table and extract information from it. They do calculations to complete the table. There is an opportunity to show how the table changes as more games are played. This can be demonstrated by you or set as an exercise for the most confident learners.

Lesson 3 (Ages 9–11)
The final games
The children examine the top and bottom of a league table with three games to go, then fill in the table again when the final results are in. They observe which teams rise to become champions and runner-up and which teams sink and are relegated.

Notes on photocopiables
Tables and results (page 61)
Questions are set on a small league table, a set of results and a table showing the effect fo the results. The answers are: 1) A; 2) B; 3) F; 4) 3, B; 5) 8, C; 6) 4, a draw; 7) B, C; 8) A; 9) 3; 10) 0; 11) 1.

Studying tables (page 62)
This sheet provides practice in reading a football table and making some simple calculations based on it. There are exercises on revising the table to take account of further results which can be done as a teacher demonstration or by the most confident learners. The answers are:

1) A; 2) E; 3) B; 4) F; 5) C; 6) B; 7) A - 30, B - 20, C - 16, D - 7, E - 8, F - 2; 8) A - 28, B - 22, C - 21, D - 19, E - 16, F - 14.

9)

| C | 9 | 8 | 0 | 1 | 28 | 8 | 20 | 24 |
| D | 10 | 6 | 1 | 3 | 37 | 34 | 3 | 19 |

10) C is now above B.

11)

| C | 10 | 8 | 0 | 2 | 31 | 12 | 19 | 24 |
| F | 10 | 5 | 2 | 3 | 27 | 24 | 3 | 17 |

12) F goes above E, C stays in the same position.

The final games (page 63)
This sheet shows how a team can rise to be champions or sink to be relegated. The answers are:

1)

Position	Team	Played	Points
1	D	46	55
2	E	46	54
3	C	46	53
4	B	46	52
5	A	46	51

2) D, E; 3 A; 4 C; 5 Y and Z;

6)

Position	Team	Played	Points
20	Z	46	29
21	Y	46	28
22	V	46	25
23	X	46	24
24	W	46	23

7) X and W.

Lesson 1 Tables and results

Resources and preparation
- Each child will need: a copy of page 61 'Tables and results', which presents some very simple data and questions about football matches. You may like to use it as a starting point, building up to other exercises related to football results and tables which extend the children's mathematical skills.
- You will also need: some football league tables from the local newspaper or football programmes.

What to do
- Talk about football results. The children may have noticed how members of their family get excited or upset after their team has played. Keep the discussion simple. Help children to understand that results and tables are important to football teams and their clubs.
- Hand out copies of page 61 and look at the first table with the children. Let them answer questions 1 to 3 on their own. You may like them to make a table on the computer.
- Look at the football results together. The word 'draw' may have arisen in your introductory discussion but if not, you may like to introduce it before the children answer the next questions. Let them answer questions 4 to 6 on their own.
- Look at the second table with the children and let them answer questions 7 to 11 on their own. You may like them to make a table on the computer.
- Review the children's answers.
- Ask the children how they would feel after the game if they were supporters of B and how they would feel if they were supporters of A.
- If the children support a local team, ask them how they feel when their team has won and when it has lost.

Extension
- The children could look at football tables in the local newspaper or in football programmes to find out the positions of various teams.
- You could point out that the tables have many more features than the ones shown on the photocopiable page, such as number of games played, number of games won, drawn or lost and goals scored for and against. The children could find out which team has drawn the most games, scored the most goals and had the most goals scored against them.

AGES 5–7

Objectives
- To learn that tables of results are produced to show how well teams are playing.
- To know that points are awarded for wins and draws but not for defeats.
- To know that teams move up and down the table according to their results.

Subject references

Mathematics
- Approach problems involving number, and data presented in a variety of forms, in order to identify what they need to do. (NC: KS1 Ma2 1a)
- Use the correct language, symbols and vocabulary associated with number and data. (NC: KS1 Ma2 1e)
- Understand addition and use related vocabulary. (NC: KS1 Ma2 3a)
- Solve a relevant problem by using simple lists, tables and charts to sort classify and organise information. (NC: KS1 Ma2 5a)

English
- Focus on the main point. (NC: KS1 En1 1d)
- Include relevant detail. (NC: KS1 En1 1e)
- Take turns in speaking. (NC: KS1 En1 3a)

ICT
- Gather information from a variety of sources. (NC: KS1 1a)
- Use tables. (NC: KS1 2a)

Lesson 2 — Studying tables

AGES 7–9

Objectives
- To be able to gather information about a team from a league table.
- To perform simple calculations to find the goal difference.
- To perform simple calculations to work out the points scored from wins and draws.
- To appreciate that the order of teams in the table may change after each game.

Subject references
Mathematics
- Identify the information needed to carry out tasks. (NC: KS2 Ma2 1b)
- Select and use appropriate mathematical equipment, including ICT. (NC: KS2 Ma2 1c)
- Choose and use an appropriate way to calculate and explain their methods and reasoning. (NC: KS2 Ma2 4b)
- Identify the data necessary to solve a given problem. (NC: KS2 Ma4 1c)
- Select and use appropriate calculation skills to solve problems involving data. (NC: KS2 Ma4 1d)

ICT
- Prepare information for development using ICT. (NC: KS2 1b)

Resources and preparation
- You will need: examples of local league tables which show how local teams are performing, access to the website of a local club.
- Each child will need: a copy of page 62 'Studying tables' and scissors.

Starter
Ask the children to explain what a league table is – it shows how well clubs are playing in comparison with each other and gives details about their performance. Ask them if they know how any of the local football clubs are performing this season and from your research give a few examples. Show the children the league table on the website of a local club. Ask them to assess the team's performance so far this season. Are they in the top half, bottom half, look as if they might be champions or relegation bound?

What to do
- Ask the children to cut out all the lines in the table and add the new lines for teams C and D to answer question 10. They should put the heading line at the top of a sheet of paper then set out the teams below it in order of the points they have.
- Explain how the goal difference is calculated and show a couple of examples on the board before letting the children try question 7.
- Explain how points are awarded for a win and a draw but not for losing and let the children try question 8.
- Tell the children that the positions of the teams in the league can change after every set of games and ask them to find out the changes to the table after just one game, the result of which is given in question 9. Steer the children towards adding an extra game to the first column and making appropriate adjustments to the other columns for teams C and D.
- Work through questions 11 and 12 with the children.
- During this work you may like the children to prepare and use tables on the computer.

LEAGUE TABLE — BARCLAYS PREMIER LEAGUE

POS	TEAM	PLD	W	D	L	F	A	GD	PTS
1	Manchester United	38	23	11	4	78	37	41	80
2	Chelsea	38	21	8	9	69	33	36	71
3	Manchester City	38	21	8	9	60	33	27	71
4	Arsenal	38	19	11	8	72	43	29	68
5	Tottenham Hotspur	38	16	14	8	55	46	9	62
6	Liverpool	38	17	7	14	59	44	15	58
7	Everton	38	13	15	10	51	45	6	54
8	Fulham	38	11	16	11	49	43	6	49
9	Aston Villa	38	12	12	14	48	59	-11	48
10	Sunderland	38	12	11	15	45	56	-11	47
11	WBA	38	12	11	15	56	71	-15	47
12	Newcastle United	38	11	13	14	56	57	-1	46
13	Stoke City	38	13	7	18	46	48	-2	46
14	Bolton	38	12	10	16	52	56	-4	46
15	Blackburn Rovers	38	11	10	17	46	59	-13	43
16	Wigan Athletic	38	9	15	14	40	61	-21	42
17	Wolverhampton	38	11	7	20	46	66	-20	40
18	Birmingham City	38	8	15	15	37	58	-21	39
19	Blackpool	38	10	9	19	55	78	-23	39
20	West Ham United	38	7	12	19	43	70	-27	33

Differentiation
- Less confident children will need help with the calculations and in ordering the teams in the table.
- More confident children could look at the local table and use questions 1 to 6 from page 62 to compare the performance of local teams.

Assessment
The children can be assessed on the accuracy of their observations of the data in the table and in their calculations. They can be assessed on how far they could change the positions of the clubs in the league without help.

Plenary
Tell the children that the tables not only show the performances of the various teams but can also be used to predict a result when two teams meet. For example, when a team at the top of the table plays one from the bottom a win for the top team might be expected. However, football predictions are often wrong because a top team can play badly or a lower team can play much better than normal. Look at a few games in the Premiership which are coming up at the weekend, look at the positions of the clubs in the table and get the class to make some predictions. After the games, the children can match the results with their predictions and assess how reliable they were.

Outcomes
- The children can gather information about a team from a league table.
- The children can perform simple calculations to find the goal difference.
- The children can perform simple calculations to work out the points scored from wins and draws.
- The children can appreciate that the order of teams in the table may change after each game.
- The children can prepare information using ICT.

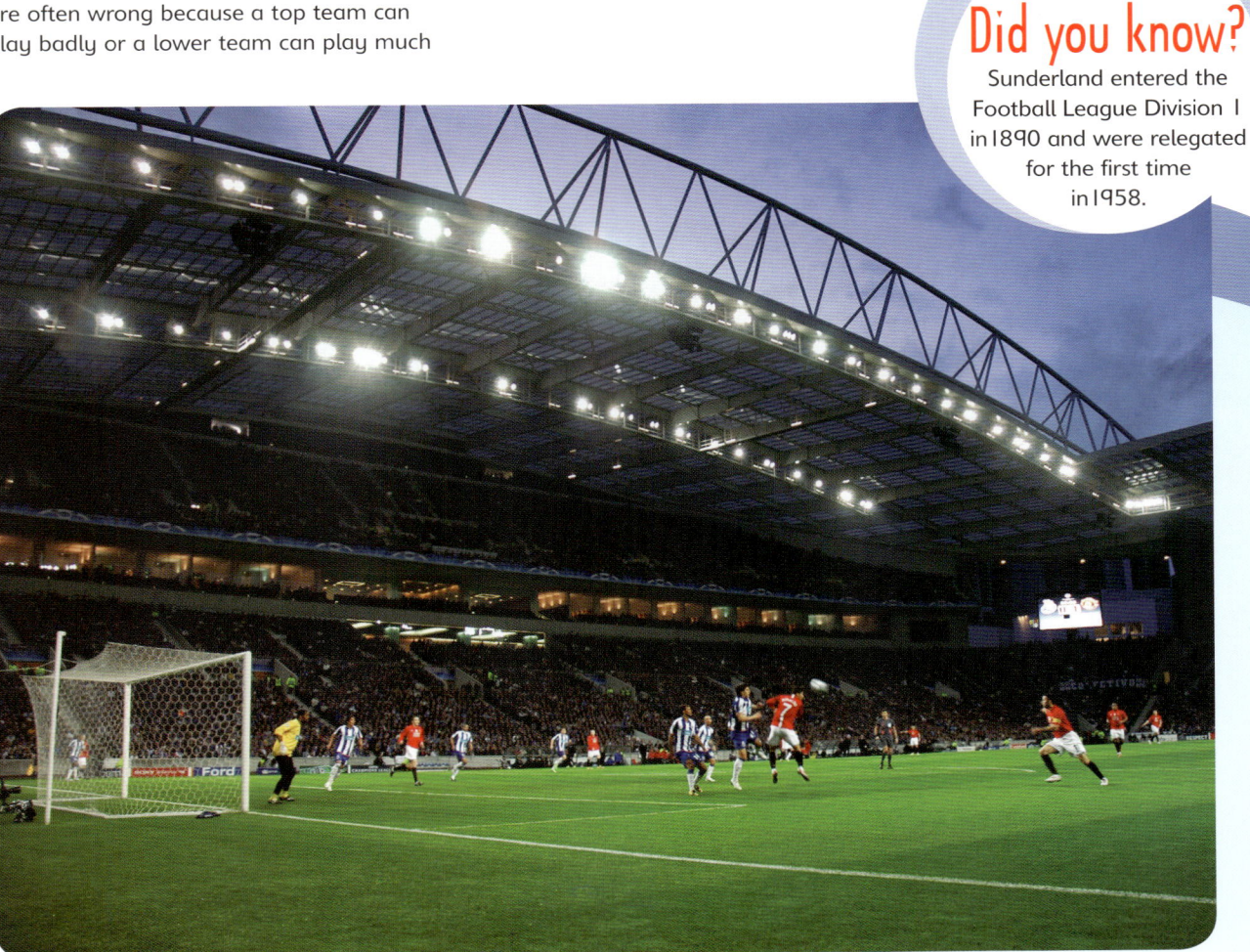

Did you know?
Sunderland entered the Football League Division 1 in 1890 and were relegated for the first time in 1958.

Lesson 3: The final games

AGES 9–11

Objectives
- To know that positions in a table can change greatly at the end of a season.
- To know the position of champions, runners up and relegated teams.

Subject references

Mathematics
- Select and use appropriate calculation skills to solve problems involving data. (NC: KS2 Ma4 1d)
- Interpret tables used in everyday life. (NC: KS2 Ma4 2b)
- Explore and use a variety of resources, including ICT. (NC: KS2 1f)

English
- Make contributions relevant to the topic and take turns in discussion. (NC: KS2 En1 3a)
- Deal politely with opposing points of view and enable discussion to move on. (NC: KS2 En1 3d)

ICT
- Prepare information for development using ICT. (NC: KS2 1b)

Resources and preparation
- Each child will need: a copy of page 63 'The final games'.
- Each group of children will need: access to a fixture list for local teams for the following Saturday and a table showing current positions for assessing the outcome of games. If possible, they should also have a form record which shows the performance of the team in the last six games.

What to do
- Ask the children how their favourite football team is doing. Ask how they know about their performance and look for an answer that mentions how league tables give details of wins, draws, losses, goals for and against, goal difference and points.
- Make sure that all the children understand how points are awarded to obtain a position in the league.
- Make sure that they know that goal difference is used when two teams have the same points, the team with the greater goal difference goes above the team with the smaller goal difference. Show the children a league table and point out goal differences. Explain that some goal differences, especially in the bottom half of the table, are negative numbers meaning that more goals have been scored against them than they have scored against other teams.
- Give out copies of page 63 and point out that in these league tables the goal differences do not apply. Ask the children to work through the questions and review their answers.
- If any child wants to talk about his or her team winning a league or being relegated, let them tell the rest of the class.
- During this work you may like the children to prepare and use tables on the computer.

Extension
- Let the children work in groups to predict the outcomes of games the following weekend by looking at the fixtures, the positions of the teams in the league and the form guide.
- From the form guide the children should decide if a team is on a winning streak or a losing run.
- Let the children discuss their predictions, giving reasons for them.
- Make sure the predictions are written down and, the following Monday, see how accurate they were.

Theme 7
Lesson 1 Tables and results

Here is a league table:

Team	Points
A	10
B	9
C	8
D	7
E	5
F	4

1. Who is at the top? _____
2. Who is second? _____
3. Who is at the bottom? _____

The teams played some more games. Here are the results:

Game 1	A 1	B 2
Game 2	C 4	D 2
Game 3	E 2	F 2

4. How many goals were scored in game 1? _____
   Who won? _____

5. How many goals were scored in game 2? _____
   What was the result? _____

6. How many goals were scored in game 3? _____
   What was the result? _____

After the games were played, the table looked like this:

Team	Points
B	12
C	11
A	10
D	7
E	6
F	5

7. Who has moved up the table? _____
8. Who has moved down the table? _____
9. How many points did B get from their game? _____
10. How many points did D get from their game? _____
11. How many points did F get from their game? _____

HOT TOPICS Football

Theme 7 Lesson 2: Studying tables

Here is the top part of a football table:

Team	Played	Won	Drawn	Lost	Goals for	Goals against	Goal difference	Points
A	10	9	1	0	40	10		
B	10	7	1	1	51	31		
C	8	7	0	1	24	8		
D	9	6	1	2	37	30		
E	10	5	1	4	28	20		
F	9	4	2	3	23	21		

1 Which team has won most games? _____

2 Which team has lost most games? _____

3 Which team has scored most goals? _____

4 Which team has scored least goals? _____

5 Which team has let in the least goals? _____

6 Which team has let in the most goals? _____

7 Find the goal difference for each team by taking away the goals against from the goals for. Write your answers in the table.

8 Find the points scored by each team by multiplying the number of games won by 3 and adding the number of games drawn. Write your answers in the table.

9 When C plays D the score is C 4 – D 0. Write new lines in the table for them here.

C								
D								

10 Cut out all the lines in the table and add these new lines for C and D.

11 When C plays F the score is C 3 – F 4. Write new lines in the table for them here.

C								
F								

12 Cut out these two lines and update your table.

Theme 7 Lesson 3 — The final games

Here is the top of a table with just three games left to play:

Position	Team	Played	Points
1	A	43	50
2	B	43	49
3	C	43	48
4	D	43	46
5	E	43	45

Position	Team	Played	Points
1			
2			
3			
4			
5			

When each club has played its final three games the points they have collected are:
A 1, B 3, C 5, D 9, E 9.

1 Update the table to find out the clubs' final positions.

2 Which teams rose the most in the last three games? _____

3 Which team dropped the most in the last three games? _____

4 Which team held their position? _____

Here is the bottom of a table with just three games to play:

Position	Team	Played	Points
20	V	43	24
21	W	43	23
22	X	43	22
23	Y	43	21
24	Z	43	20

Position	Team	Played	Points
20			
21			
22			
23			
24			

5 The bottom two clubs at the end of the season will be relegated. Which clubs are in the relegation positions in the table? _____

When each club has played its last three games the points they have collected are:
V 1, W 0, X 2, Y 7 and Z 9.

6 Fill in the final details about the bottom of the table.

7 Which teams were relegated? _____

HOT TOPICS Football

Theme 8: Football around the world

BACKGROUND

England and Scotland are the joint oldest national football teams in the world. The first international match was played in 1870 at the Oval (famous now as a cricket ground) and the result was a 1-1 draw.

Wales are the third oldest national football team in the world and played their first international match in 1872 against Scotland in Glasgow. Scotland won 4-0. The following year the return match was the first international football match to take place in Wales (at Wrexham) and Scotland won again 2-0.

The Northern Ireland team, originally the Ireland National football team from 1882 to 1950, was the fourth oldest national football team in the world. Their first international game against England in 1882 in Belfast resulted in a 13-0 defeat and England's greatest ever win.

THE CONTENTS

Lesson 1 (Ages 5–7)
The national teams of the UK
The children learn about the national flags of England, Scotland, Wales and Northern Ireland and the football strip of each team.

Lesson 2 (Ages 7–9)
Where do players come from?
The children look at the squad of a selected team or teams and find out where each player comes from. They select six countries and find out about the strip worn by each country in international matches and the flag waved by supporters.

Lesson 3 (Ages 9–11)
Football around the world
The children read about the spread of football around the world, the early development of FIFA and look at a map showing the six global regions of football that exist today. They use the internet to find player profiles and their nationalities. They discover the strips of different countries, colour them onto outlines of players and place them in the correct football regions.

Notes on photocopiables

The national teams of the UK (page 69)
This sheet features four flags and players' strips to be coloured in to represent each of the four nations in the United Kingdom.

Where do players come from? (page 70)
This sheet features six flags and players' strips to be coloured in to represent six countries around the world which compete in international competitions.

Football around the world (page 71)
This page features a brief explanation of how modern football spread out from the United Kingdom to the rest of the world and describes the early development of FIFA. A map of the world showing the six global regions can be used for matching national strips to countries. The image below shows the national flags of the 32 nations that played in the 2010 World Cup in South Africa.

Lesson 1: The national teams of the UK

Resources and preparation
- Each child will need: a copy of page 69 'The national teams of the UK' and a map of the British Isles.
- You will need: a wallchart map of the British Isles clearly showing England, Scotland, Wales and Northern Ireland, the national flags of all four countries and images of players wearing the national strip.
- There are pictures of the English, Scottish and Welsh flags at the website: www.flags-flags-flags.org.uk
- Northern Ireland does not have a national flag but some supporters use the Ulster banner, a red cross with the hand of Ulster and the crown at the centre.
- You may find photos of players wearing the national strips in football magazines or newspaper sports sections or you could search on the internet.

What to do
- Show the children a map of the British Isles and point out where they live. Ask them which country of the United Kingdom they live in.
- Tell the children that each country has its own football team and some supporters take their national flags to international matches. Make sure the children understand that an international match is played between two different countries. Show the children the four flags of England, Scotland, Wales and Northern Ireland.
- If you have stressed the importance of rules and fair play when playing football you might like to extend these ideas to the flags, saying that the colours used in heraldry and club badges have special meanings. For example, white represents honesty and peace, red represents bravery and strength, blue represents justice and truth. These meanings can be used to guide players in any sport. The Northern Ireland 'flag' (also called the Ulster Banner) is red and white. It has a crown to show loyalty to the royal family and the Red Hand of Ulster whose origin goes back to myths and legends about kings or giants who lost a hand in battle.
- Hand out copies of page 69 and display pictures of the England strip. Let the children colour in one of the players. Display the England flag and let the children colour in the flag next to the player.
- Repeat this activity with the strips and flags for Scotland, Wales and Northern Ireland.

Extension
Remind the children where the four nations of the British Isles are found and hand out copies of the map. Let the children decide how they could present the information about each player, flag and country. For example, they could cut out the flags, mount them on sticks and place them above the country with the player close by.

AGES 5–7

Objectives
- To learn about the flags of the United Kingdom.
- To learn about the colours and designs of the kit belonging to the four national football teams.
- To colour in the flags and designs neatly.
- To link the flags and kits with the locations of the four nations in the British Isles.

Subject references

Geography
- Use maps at a range of scales. (NC: KS1 2c)
- Identify and describe where places are. (NC: KS1 3b)
- Recognise how places compare with other places. (NC: KS1 3d)

English
- Use adventurous and wide-ranging vocabulary. (NC: KS1 En3 1a)

Design and technology
- Develop ideas by shaping materials and putting together components. (NC: KS1 1b)

Lesson 2 — Where do players come from?

AGES 7–9

Objectives
- To learn about the flags of countries with international football teams.
- To learn about the colours and designs of international football strips.
- To colour in the flags and designs neatly.
- To link the flags and strips with the locations of countries around the world.

Subject references

Geography
- Use atlases and globes at a range of scales. (NC: KS2 2c)
- Study a range of places in different parts of the world. (NC: KS2 7b)

ICT
- Prepare information for development using ICT, including selecting sources, finding information, classifying it and checking it for accuracy. (NC: KS2 1b)
- Work with others to explore a variety of information sources and ICT. (NC: KS2 5b)

Resources and preparation
- Before the lesson, you will need to look at the website of a local or favourite club and find the team information using the information bar. Scroll to 'profiles' and look through the squad to find where each player comes from. Alternatively, use the National Football Teams website at:
www.national-football-teams.com/v2/leagues.php?id=59
This gives you the country of origin of every player at a given club. If you click on the country of origin it shows you the strip used by the outfield players.
- You will need: a map of the United Kingdom with the countries clearly marked, maps of Europe and the world, a range of resources showing the flags of the countries of the world. This can include books, wallcharts and wesbites.
- You will also need plenty of helpers to assist the children in using the internet.
- Each child will need: a copy of page 70 'Where do players come from'.
- Each group of children will need: a copy of a world map.

Starter
- Show the children a map of the United Kingdom with the four countries clearly marked and ask them to say in which country they live.
- Show the children a map of Europe. Explain that some people go on holiday in Europe to places such as France, Spain and Italy and point to these places.
- Show the children a map of the world and say that some people go even further and point out Florida in the United States of America and Thailand. Say that the football game we play today spread out from the United Kingdom around the world and many players from other countries now play for our teams.

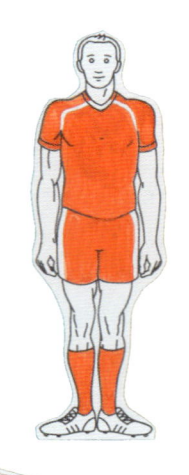

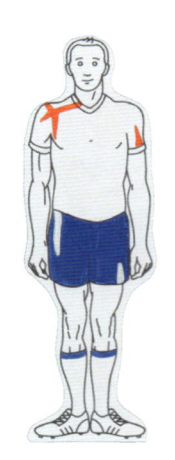

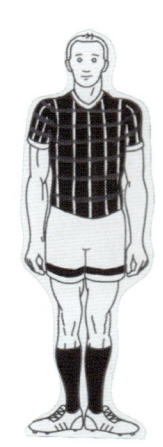

66

What to do

- Hand out copies of page 70 and tell the children they are going to find out where different football players come from.
- Visit the website of your local team or a favourite club to find the team section and look at a player profile. It will show a photograph of the player and their details, including nationality. Use this information to find the country on the map.
- Use your resources about flags to help the children find the country's flag. They could colour in the flag next to one of the players on the photocopiable page.
- Tell the children that the player might not have played for their country in internationals but they are going to find out about the strip that the players wear. Go to the website www.national-football-teams.com/v2/leagues.php?id=59 and click on the club. Find the player and click on his land of origin to find the design of the strip. The children can then colour in the player alongside the flag.
- Let the children use the website to find out about other players and colour in five more flags and strips.

Differentiation

The less confident learners will need help in locating the flags and strips. The more confident learners could, after colouring in the strip for a country, look down the squad list to identify players who play for clubs in England, Scotland, Wales and Northern Ireland.

Assessment

The children could be assessed on the presentation of their flags and strips. They could also be assessed on the ease with which they use the internet to access information and complete their tasks.

Plenary

The children could cut out their players and flags, paste them around a world map and draw label lines from each player to the location of the country they represent.

Outcomes

- The children learn about the flags of countries with international football teams.
- They learn about the colours and designs of international football strips.
- They colour in the flags and designs neatly.
- They can match the flags and kits to the locations of countries around the world.

Lesson 3: Football around the world

AGES 9–11

Objectives
- To learn how football spread out from the United Kingdom.
- To recognise the six global groups for national football teams.
- To learn about the flags and kits of international football teams.

Subject references

Geography
- Use atlases and globes at a range of scales. (NC: KS2 2c)
- Study a range of places in different parts of the world. (NC: KS2 7b)

History
- Place events, people and changes in correct periods of time. (NC: KS2 1a)
- Communicate their knowledge and understanding of history in a variety of ways. (NC: KS2 5c)

ICT
- Prepare information for development using ICT, including selecting sources, finding information, classifying it and checking it for accuracy. (NC: KS2 1b)
- Work with others to explore a variety of information sources and ICT. (NC: KS2 5b)

Resources and preparation
- You will need: the timeline from Theme 1, Lessons 2 and 3, a large map of the world mounted on card.
- The children will need: copies of page 71 'Football around the world', coloured paper, cocktail sticks and sticky tape (to make flags), copies of page 70 to colour in, access to the website of their local or favourite football team and the National Football Teams website at www.national-football-teams.com/v2/leagues.php?id=59. This lists the country of origin of every player at a given club. Click on the country of origin to see the strip used by the outfield players of that country.

What to do
- Hand out copies of page 71 and read through the text with the children. Ask them to make flags to stick on the timeline showing when the various countries joined FIFA.
- Let the children look at the websites of their local or favourite football teams. Click on the team section and search through the player profiles to find the nationalities of the players.
- Tell the children that they can also find out about the nationalities of players at the National Football Teams website by clicking on their club. Let them look at this website to find out more about the strips of various international sides. Click on the country of origin to see the strip used by the outfield players of that country in international matches.
- When the children know how to locate international strips, ask them to find them them for Australia, China and Pakistan (AFC), Kenya, Nigeria and South Africa (CAF), Jamaica, Mexico, United States (CONCACAF), Argentina, Brazil, Uruguay (CONMEBOL), Fiji, New Zealand and Tonga (OFC), France, Germany and Italy (UEFA). They can colour in the strips of one of the countries in each group on their copy of page 70, and place a label about the country next to each player.

Extension
- Set out the map of the world mounted on card and let some children colour-code the areas of the six global football groups.
- Let other children cut out their players in international kits and stick them on the map in or near the regions in which they play. Let them use atlases to locate the countries on the world map and draw lines from the players to the countries for which they play.

Did you know?
Brazil is the only country to have had a team in every World Cup tournament.

Theme 8 Lesson 1: The national teams of the UK

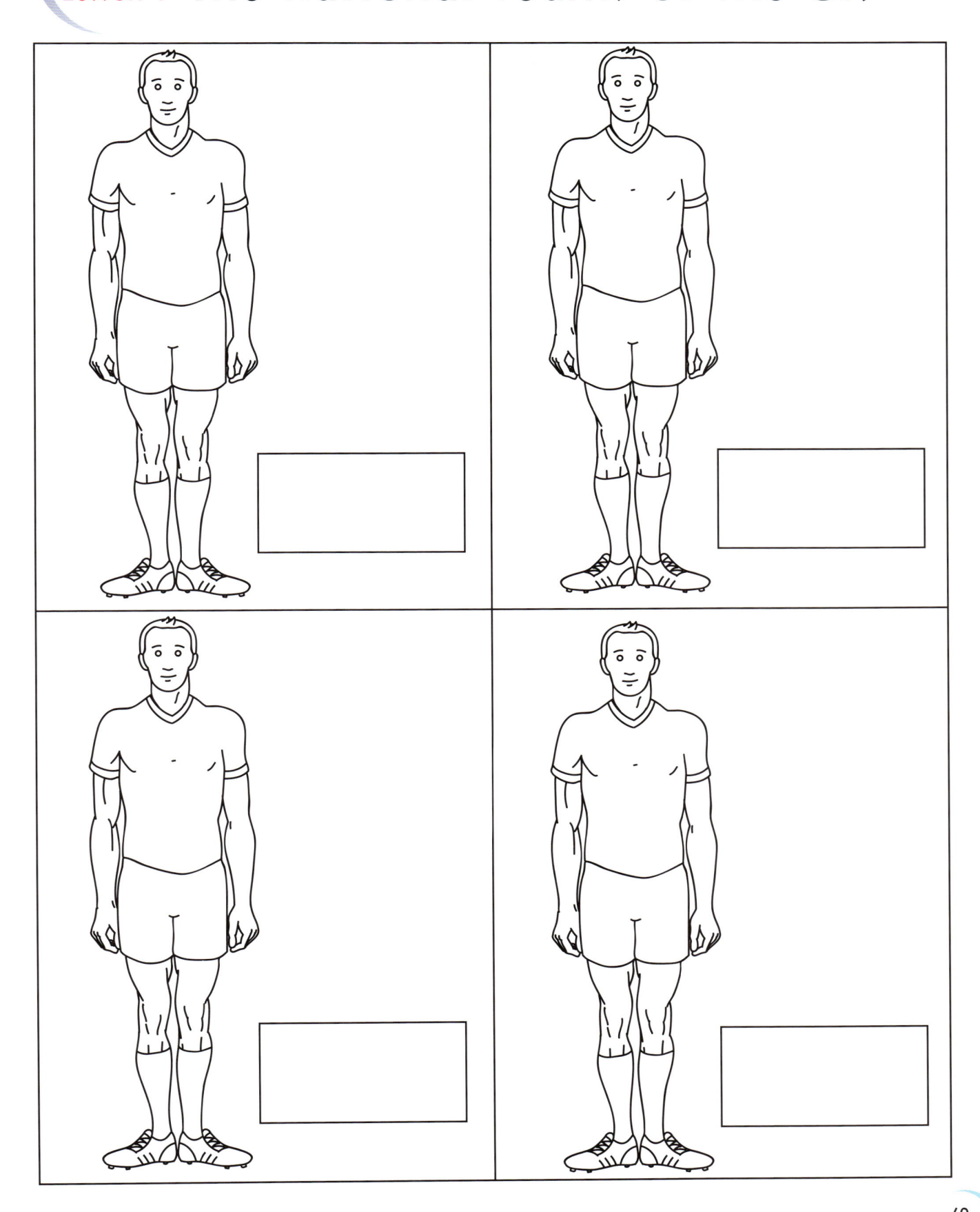

HOT TOPICS Football

Theme 8 Lesson 2
Where do players come from?

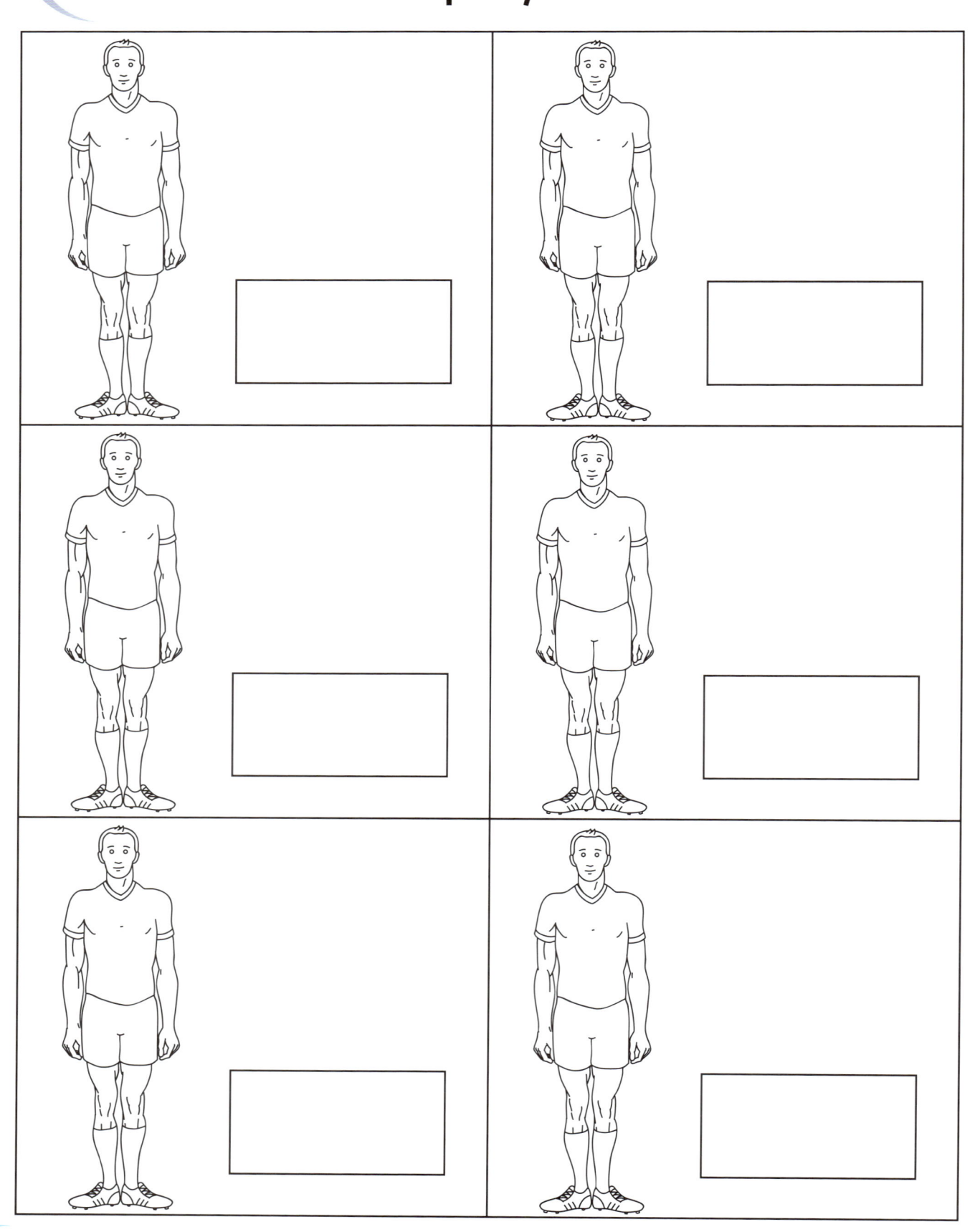

Theme 8 Lesson 3: Football around the world

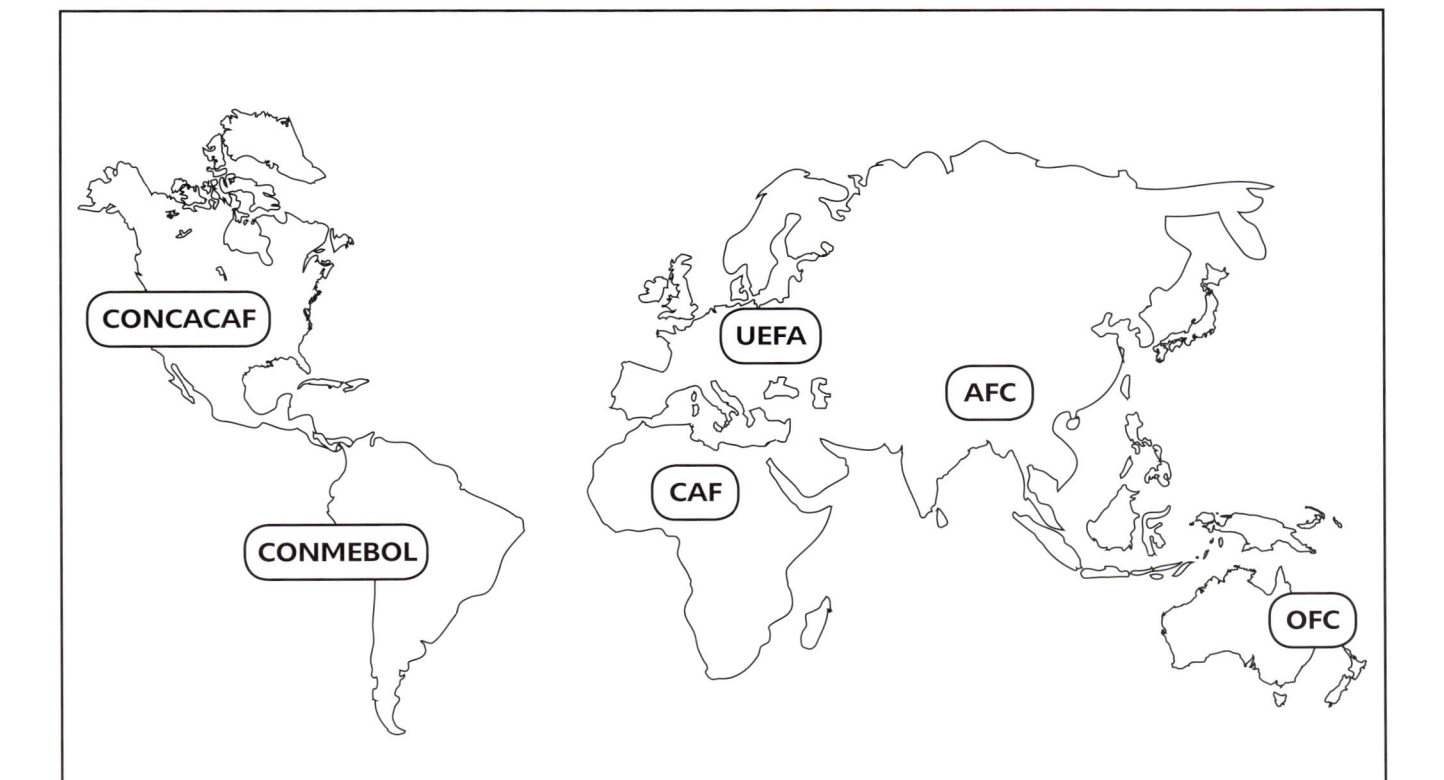

[Map showing the six FIFA confederations: CONCACAF, CONMEBOL, UEFA, CAF, AFC, OFC]

The United Kingdom was where modern football began because it was here that the rules of the game were set down. When UK citizens travelled to other parts of the world, either with the military forces or in connection with their work, they would play the game and it was not long before the locals began to play it too.

Eventually national associations were set up in countries across the world similar to the Football Association in England. By 1904 there was a need to organise the national associations for international matches and the *Fédération Internationale de Football Association* (FIFA) was founded in Paris. The first member countries were France, Belgium, Denmark, the Netherlands, Spain, Sweden and Switzerland. In 1905 England, Scotland, Wales, Ireland, Austria, Germany, Italy and Hungary joined.

At first, only European clubs were included but in 1909 South Africa joined, followed by Chile and Argentina in 1912 and the USA in 1913.

As more countries set up their own national associations and joined FIFA they were divided into six global groups, as shown on the map.

KEY to abbreviations:
CONCACAF
Confederation of North, Central American and Caribbean Association Football
CONMEBOL
Confederación Sudamericana de Futbol in South America
CAF
Confédération Africaine de Football in Africa
UEFA
Union of European Football Associations
AFC
Asian Football Confederation
OFC
Oceania Football Confederation

HOT TOPICS Football

Theme 9 Competitions

BACKGROUND

The oldest domestic football competition in the world is the FA Cup. Its proper title is the Football Association Challenge Cup. The competition was first held in the 1871–1872 season. The first cup was stolen in 1895, the second was used until 1910, and the third until 1992 when the fourth cup, currently in use, was introduced.

Before the final, the ribbons of both clubs are attached to the cup and those of the losing team are removed at the end of the match. This competition is open to the Premiership, Football League (Championship, League 1 and League 2) and a further six lower divisions.

As football grounds became equipped with floodlights it was decided to introduce a mid-week competition in the 1960–61 season called the League Cup. This is open to Premiership and Football League clubs and now carries the name of the competition sponsor. For example, in recent years it has been known as the Coca-Cola Cup, the Worthington Cup and the Carling Cup. The original trophy is presented to the winners.

The World Cup developed from football competitions which took place at the Olympics from 1908 until 1928. Jules Rimet, who was president of FIFA, was primarily responsible for turning the idea of a world cup competition into a reality and the first World Cup trophy was named after him. When Brazil won the cup for the third time they were allowed to keep it and a new cup was made called the FIFA World Cup Trophy.

THE CONTENTS

Lesson 1 (Ages 5–7)
Come on Football!
The children learn a football song and develop a stage performance to accompany it.

Lesson 2 (Ages 7–9)
Cups, medals and caps
The children design and make a model cup, a winner's medal and a football cap. They re-enact an awards ceremony.

Lesson 3 (Ages 9–11)
The World Cup
The children cut out the dates and venues of the World Cup and match them to the countries on a map. They devise and take part in a World Cup quiz.

Notes on photocopiables

Football song (page 77)
Words and music to a football song, 'Come on football!' are provided.

Cups, medals and caps (page 78)
This page provides pictures of the FA cup, two sides of a winner's medal and a football cap.

World Cup timeline (page 79)
This page features dates, venues and final results of the World Cup competitions.

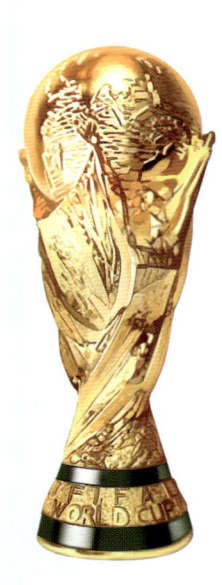

Lesson 1 — Come on football!

Resources and preparation
- Each child will need: a copy of page 77 'Come on football!' with the words to the football song.
- If you are going to perform actions to accompany the song, you will need: for verse 1 an old leather football, medieval peasant costumes for mob football; for verse 2 a referee's uniform with watch and whistle, two assistant referees' uniforms (linesmen/women) with two yellow flags; for verse 3 the children could wear the kits of their favourite football teams and carry footballs. Some children could form a crowd of supporters, wearing ordinary clothes with scarves and hats; one could beat a drum.

What to do
- Tell the children that crowds have always gathered to watch football matches and cheer the teams on. Some clubs have songs associated with their team. One of the most famous is 'You'll never walk alone' which is sung by supporters of Liverpool Football Club. Fans at matches often chant, accompanied by clapping.
- Hand out page 77 and tell the children they are going to learn a football song and work out actions for it.
- Practise the song together then, if you wish to perform actions, follow the suggestions in the extension.

Extension
- For the introductory two lines of chorus, let some children dress as football supporters with scarves and hats. One child can beat a rhythm on the drum.
- Verse 1 is a mob football scene. The children can dress in medieval peasant costumes and softly run around the stage after a child carrying an old football.
- In each chorus the supporters can clap to the beat of the drum.
- In verse 2, the referee and assistant referees can burst onto the stage to bring order to the proceedings. The referee looks at their watch and blows their whistle; assistant referees can wave their flags, perhaps in rhythm.
- For verse 3 the children, dressed as footballers, run onto the stage. They could demonstrate some basic football skills.

AGES 5–7

Objectives
- To learn a song.
- To develop actions to accompany the song.
- To perform the song and actions to an audience.

Subject references

Music
- Use their voices expressively by singing songs and speaking chants. (NC: KS1 1a)
- Rehearse and perform with others. (NC: KS1 1c)
- Explore and express their ideas and feelings about music using movement, dance and expressive and musical language. (NC: KS1 3a)

Physical education
- Use movement imaginatively, responding to stimuli, including music and performing basic skills. (NC: KS1 6a)

English
- Use language and actions to explore and convey situations, characters and emotions. (NC: KS1 4a)
- Create and sustain roles individually and when working with others. (NC: KS1 4b)

Did you know?
Stanley Matthews (1915 – 2000) was the first footballer to be knighted (in 1965).

Lesson 2 Cups, medals and caps

AGES 7–9

Objectives
- To learn that football achievements are recognised by the awarding of trophies, medals and caps.
- To design and make a cup, medal or cap.

Subject references

Design and technology
- Develop ideas and explain them clearly, putting together a list of what they want their design to achieve. (NC: KS2 1b)
- Plan what they have to do, suggesting a sequence of actions and alternatives if needed. (NC: KS2 1c)
- Reflect on the progress of their work as they design and make, identifying ways they could improve their products. (NC: KS2 3a)

English
- Create, adapt and sustain different roles, individually and in groups. (NC: KS2 En1 4a)

Resources and preparation
- For the starter, you will need: a school trophy cabinet, examples of sports medals.
- Each child or group will need copies of page 78 'Cups, medals and caps' and, according to their choice: modelling clay, plastic knives and silver paint to make a cup; cardboard discs, ribbon, glue and scissors to make a medal; a simple cap with a tassel and cord (or materials for making a tassel), braid, cardboard for making a badge, scissors and glue.

Starter
If your school has a display cabinet in the entrance hall, take the children to look at it. Take out some of the trophies and show them to the children. Point out that trophies can take the form of cups or shields. It does not matter if the trophies are for music as the principle is the same – they recognise a level of achievement. Show the children some medals which have been issued to people for taking part in an event. Point out that medals are awards for winners and for runners up.

What to do
- Hand out copies of page 78 and say that in football any team winning a competition is awarded a trophy, usually a cup, while the players receive medals. Players who take part in international matches are given a football cap to mark the occasion. Caps were worn in the early days of football when players did not have a football kit with team colours – they could wear what they liked. Players in each team wore the same hats to distinguish themselves from their opponents. These hats often took the form of caps and the tradition of awarding caps for internationals began.
- Tell the children that they are going to design and make cups (from modelling clay), make medals (from pieces of circular card and ribbons) and decorate caps. They can use the information on page 78 to help them.
- The children should draw out their designs on paper first and discuss them with you then use the materials to make their chosen object.

Differentiation
- Less confident learners will need help shaping the clay and making and attaching the items to a cap.
- More confident learners can use plastic knives to carve designs in their cups or make their own tassels and braid.

Assessment
The children can be assessed on the intricacy of the detail on their cups, the design on the back of the medal and the final appearance of the cap.

Plenary
The children can display their items in class or in a display cabinet in the school entrance. If the children have made enough caps and medals they could devise and take part in an awards ceremony. Two children can hold trays of caps and medals. Choose someone to present the caps and another to award the medals. The 'players' can line up wearing their caps and medals.

Outcomes
- The children learn that football achievements are recognised by the awarding of trophies, medals and caps.
- They can design and make a cup, medal or cap.

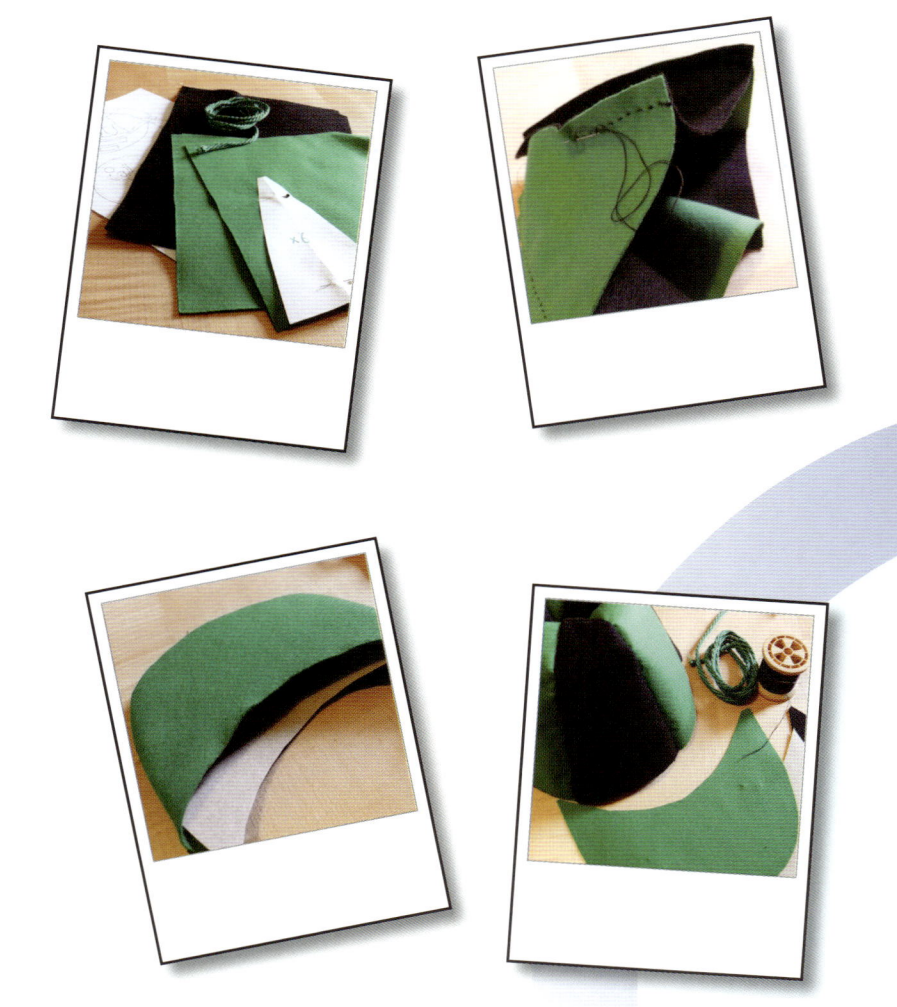

Lesson 3 — The World Cup

AGES 9–11

Objectives
- To learn about the history of the World Cup.
- To learn about the location of World Cup competitions.
- To construct and use a football quiz.

Subject references

History
- Describe and make links between main events across societies studied. (NC: KS2 2d)
- Recall, select and organise historical information. (NC: KS2 5a)

Geography
- Use atlases at a range of scales. (NC: KS2 2c)
- Describe where places are. (NC: KS2 3c)
- Study a range of places in different parts of the world. (NC: KS2 7b)

English
- Choose form and content to suit a particular purpose. (NC: KS2 En3 1a)
- Use language and style that are appropriate to the reader. (NC: KS2 En3 1c)

Resources and preparation
- Each child will need a copy of page 79 'World Cup timeline'. (Point out that West Germany became known as Germany after East and West Germany were reunited and that the Netherlands is the correct name for a country that is often called Holland.)
- Each group of children will need: an outline map of the world, mounted on card, to which the information blocks can be pasted, an atlas, scissors, glue.

What to do
- Remind the children how football spread around the world (Theme 8 Lesson 3). Tell them that a football competition was introduced into the Olympic Games in 1908 and by 1928 FIFA decided to develop a separate World Cup competition. As Uruguay had won two of the Olympic competitions and the country was celebrating its centenary in 1930 it was decided to hold the first World Cup competition there.
- Hand out copies of page 79 and let the children look through the information. Point out that World Cup competitions were not held in the 1940s during World War II.
- Give the children outline maps of the world and atlases and let them find the countries in which the competitions have taken place.
- Let the children cut out each block of information from page 79 and paste it around the world map and draw a line between it and the country.

Extension
There are many quiz books on football and some people pride themselves on their football knowledge. Let groups of children produce World Cup quiz sheets based on the information provided on page 79. Questions could range from who has won the World Cup the most times to how many games have been decided on penalties. Pairs of teams could take part in a competition, deciding between themselves how to award marks when both teams have the same question.

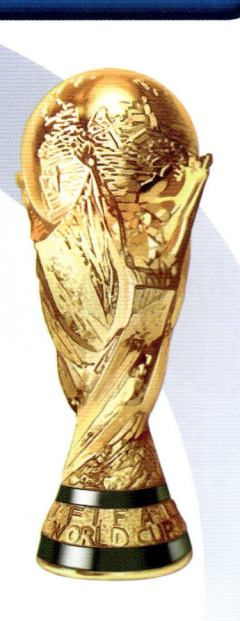

2010 FIFA World Cup stadium in Capetown, South Africa

Come on football!

Theme 9 – Lesson 1

Come on football!

clap clap *shake shake*
SHOOT! SAVE! SAVE! SHOOT!
clap clap *shake shake*
GOAL!

When we first played foot-ball, we kicked it ev-'ry where.
Ref is in the mid-dle, he's loo-king at the time.
Lots of clubs to fol-low, there's lots of games to play.

O-ver fields and ri-vers, we di-dn't have a care.
Whis-tle blows, off we go, his mates run on the line.
Cups and caps and me-dals, let's win 'em all, Hor-ray!

clap clap *shake shake*
SHOOT! SAVE! SAVE! SHOOT!
clap clap *shake shake*
GOAL!

clap clap *shake shake*
SHOOT! SAVE! SAVE! SHOOT!
clap clap *shake shake*
GOAL!

1) When we first played football
   We kicked it everywhere
   Over fields and rivers
   We didn't have a care

2) Now the ref is in the middle
   Looking at the time
   Whistle blows of we go
   His mates run on the line

3) There's lots of clubs to follow
   There's lots of games to play
   There's cups and caps and medals
   Lets win 'em all, Horray!

Music by Sally-Ann Riley. Words by Peter Riley

HOT TOPICS Football

Theme 9 Lesson 2: Cups, medals and caps

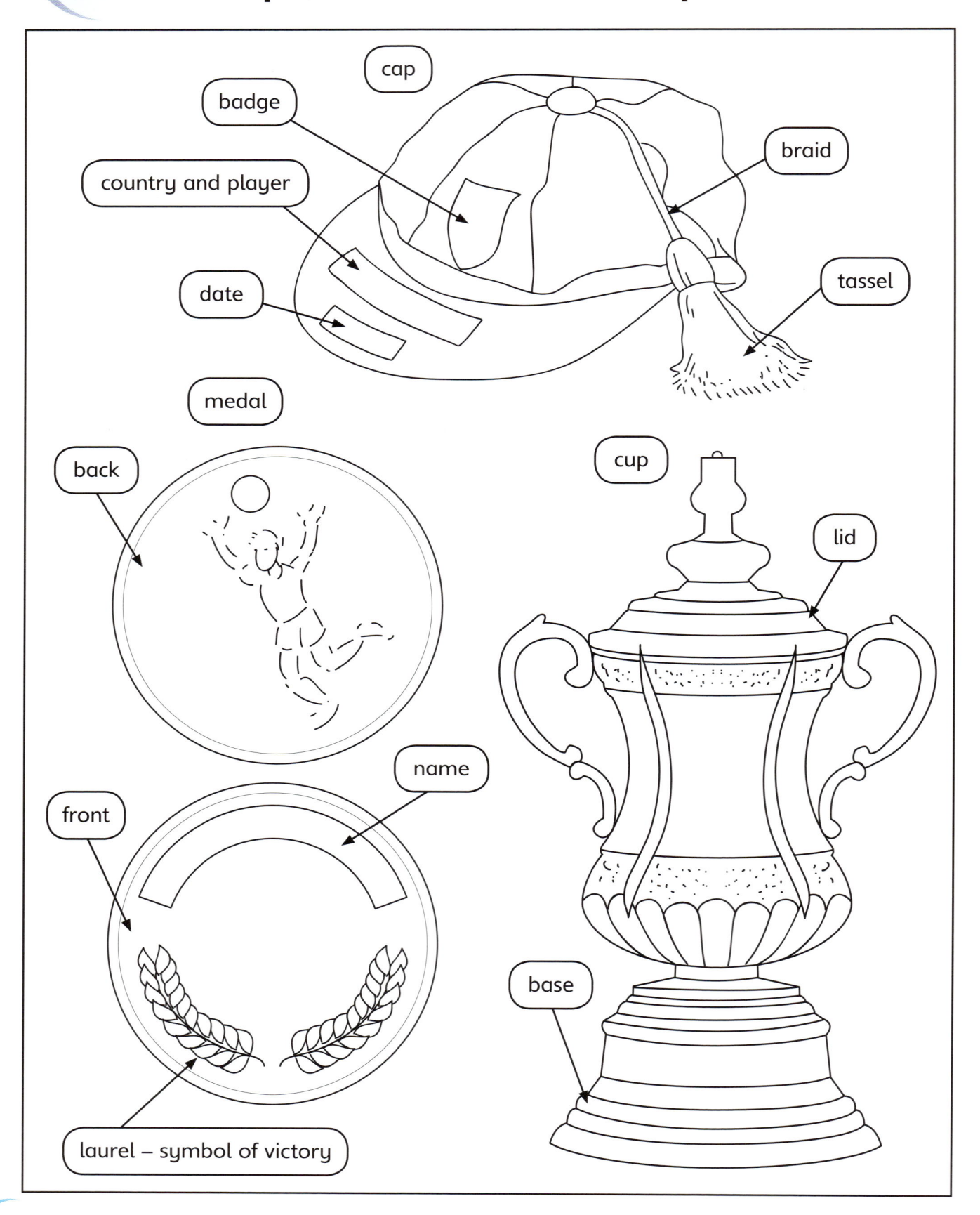

cap — (hat)
- badge
- country and player
- date
- braid
- tassel

medal
- back
- front
- name
- laurel – symbol of victory

cup
- lid
- base

HOT TOPICS Football

World Cup timeline

Theme 9 Lesson 3

1930 *Uruguay* Uruguay 4 Argentina 2	**1934** *Italy* Italy 2 Czechoslovakia 1	**1938** *France* Italy 4 Hungary 2	**1950** *Brazil* Uruguay 2 Brazil 1
1954 *Switzerland* West Germany 3 Hungary 2	**1958** *Sweden* Brazil 5 Sweden 2	**1962** *Chile* Brazil 3 Czechoslovakia 1	**1966** *England* England 4 West Germany 2
1970 *Mexico* Brazil 4 Italy 1	**1974** *West Germany* West Germany 2 Netherlands 1	**1978** *Argentina* Argentina 3 Netherlands 1	**1982** *Spain* Italy 3 West Germany 1
1986 *Mexico* Argentina 3 West Germany 2	**1990** *Italy* West Germany 1 Argentina 0	**1994** *United States* Brazil 3 Italy 2 (after penalties)	**1998** *France* France 3 Brazil 0
2002 *South Korea and Japan* Brazil 2 Germany 0	**2006** *Germany* Italy 5 France 3 (after penalties)	**2010** *South Africa* Spain 1 Netherlands 0	**2014** *Brazil*

HOT TOPICS Football

SCHOLASTIC

In this series:

Castles
978-0439-94510-3 (Book)
978-1407-12232-8 (CD-ROM)

Dinosaurs
978-0439-94509-7 (Book)
978-1407-12233-5 (CD-ROM)

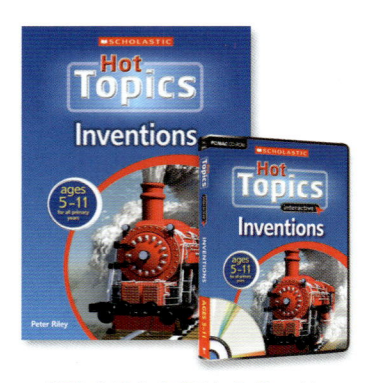

Inventions
978-0439-94511-0 (Book)
978-1407-12234-2 (CD-ROM)

Olympics
978-0439-94573-8 (Book)
978-1407-12235-9 (CD-ROM)

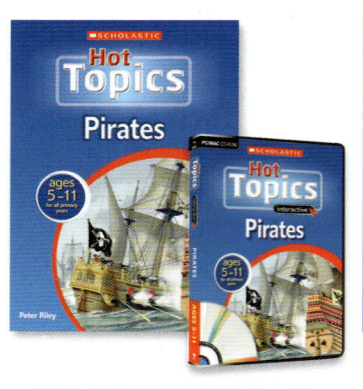

Pirates
978-0439-94552-3 (Book)
978-1407-12236-6 (CD-ROM)

Space
978-0439-94574-5 (Book)
978-1407-12238-0 (CD-ROM)

Rainforests
ISBN 978-0439-94553-0 (Book)
978-1407-12237-3 (CD-ROM)

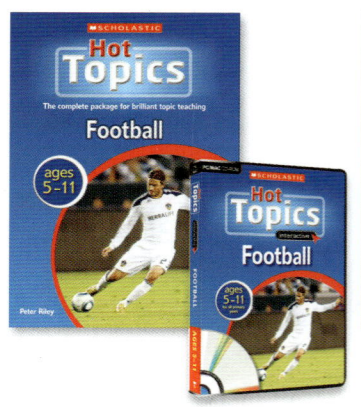

Football
978-1407-12710-1 (Book)
978-1407-12714-9 (CD-ROM)

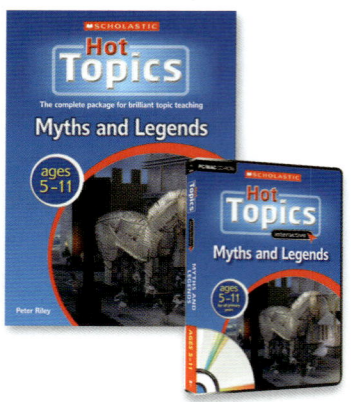

Myths and Legends
978-1407-12713-2 (Book)
978-1407-12717-0 (CD-ROM)

Habitats
978-1407-12712-5 (Book)
978-1407-12716-3 (CD-ROM)

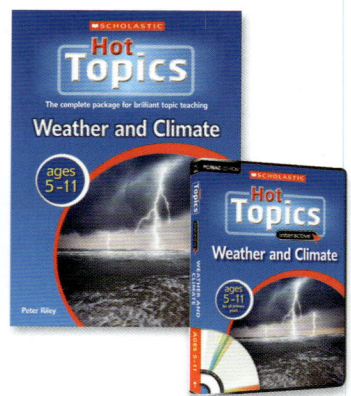

Weather and Climate
978-1407-12711-8 (Book)
978-1407-12715-6 (CD-ROM)

To find out more, call: **0845 603 9091**
or visit **www.scholastic.co.uk**